The Commons in History

History for a Sustainable Future
Michael Egan, series editor

Derek Wall, *The Commons in History: Culture, Conflict, and Ecology*
Frank Uekötter, *The Greenest Nation? A New History of German Environmentalism*

The Commons in History

Culture, Conflict, and Ecology

Derek Wall

The MIT Press
Cambridge, Massachusetts
London, England

First MIT Press paperback edition, 2017

© 2014 Massachusetts Institute of Technology

This book was set in Sabon by the MIT Press.

Library of Congress Cataloging-in-Publication Data

Wall, Derek.
The commons in history : culture, conflict, and ecology / Derek Wall.
   pages   cm. —(History for a sustainable future)
Includes bibliographical references and index.
ISBN 978-0-262-02721-2 (hardcover : alk. paper), 978-0-262-53470-3 (pb.)
1. Commons—History. I. Title.
HD1286.W34   2014
333.2—dc23
2013032414

To Emily Blyth and Amanda Penfold

What we need to question is bricks, concrete, glass, our table manners, our utensils, our tools, the way we spend our time, our rhythms. To question that which seems to have ceased forever to astonish us. We live, true, we breathe, true; we walk, we go downstairs, we sit at a table in order to eat, we lie down on a bed in order to sleep. How? Where? When? Why?

Describe your street. Describe another. Compare.

—Georges Perec, *L'Infra-ordinaire* (1989)

Contents

Foreword

Michael Egan

Derek Wall's *The Commons in History: Culture, Conflict, and Ecology* inaugurates a new series from the MIT Press. "History for a Sustainable Future" is predicated on the idea that scholars, publics, and policymakers need to be conscious of the historical contexts of contemporary environmental problems to understand their social, political, economic, and ecological contexts. Resolving local and global environmental quandaries requires careful thought and planning, and future success depends on a deep appreciation of the past. This is the point of the series: we can learn from past mistakes, but more important, solving the environmental crisis demands the best information available, and history provides valuable insights into the creation and proliferation of the environmental ills we hope to curb.

Fittingly, the commons in history is a good departure point for this series for two reasons. First, the commons constitutes one of the oldest stories of human interaction with the physical environment. The collective use of land and extraction of resources has been engrained in human activities since before history was written down. Second, this story possesses critical contemporary relevance for helping us to move toward a more sustainable future. As Wall notes in his introduction to this book, understanding property rights is essential for understanding sustainability. How we use, share, close off, and open up the land and its resources offers insights into how we value the environment, the economy, and each other. And by applying an historical lens to how the commons have evolved over time and across space, Wall reads a method of engaging with the future.

Wall examines the historical commons to determine what we can learn from the past and how we might use it to inform future deliberations. In so doing, Wall champions the commons but criticizes their enclosure. A *commons* is land that is set aside for public use and jointly owned and managed by its surrounding community. *Use* is the key word here. As Brian Donahue notes, "to have a real commons [is] something more than enjoying a park, in other words, more than tossing a frisbee on the town green"; it requires some means of "productive economic engagement."[1] By extension, *enclosure* (or the blocking of access to commons through the establishment of private property or legal restrictions imposed on some members of the public) constitutes another form of productive economic engagement, but it often comes at the expense of a broader public good. In this respect, when we talk about managing nature, we are talking about managing people, which introduces questions of power and the unequal distribution of access to resources.

As Wall demonstrates, the commons has multiple personalities. In overlapping scenarios, it is a material space organized by a form of local self-governance, an economic abstraction that explores collective resource use, and a practical tool for resource management. More recent practices have also developed a creative commons, which expands the intellectual resources of the information age and can be applied to the production of new ideas, work, and things. As the futurist and technology activist Stewart Brand famously asserted, "Information wants to be free."[2] If blueprints, open-source software, and free and collaborative knowledge collection mark a new era for the information age, then how might we reimagine a transformation of the physical commons by examining it historically?

This question is complicated by the conflicting baggage that travels with the commons as an idea, as an ecological space, and as a management practice. According to its analysts, it is either preternaturally good or intrinsically bad. For its proponents, the commons engenders notions of economic equality, ecological responsibility, and social justice while it encourages community, support, and the collective production of goods. For its detractors, the commons are a naïve and outdated system of land management that fails to address the increasing demands for resources in a growth-driven economy and is wholly inconsistent with the four P's of capitalism—property, productivity, profit, and progress. In a recent study on the "cosmopolitan commons," Nil Disco and Eda Kranakis observe the ahistorical tension in this duality and the importance of situating the commons in time and place.[3]

This is what Wall does. Throughout *The Commons in History*, Wall emphasizes that the commons are culturally designed and historically dynamic and that most commons are never put to the test on their own merits. Instead, they are typically enclosed and turned over to private owners For Wall, this is the true tragedy of the commons. His book weaves culture and politics into the traditional economic framework that drives much work on the commons. His wide-ranging examples reveal a certain consistency in the historical analysis.

Sustainability implies hope, and Wall's history seems to point toward a hopeful rehabilitation of the commons. Since the 1960s, the commons has been derided by neo-Malthusians as a wildly problematic method of land management. Garrett Hardin's famous essay "The Tragedy of the Commons" (1968) ushered in a new wave of commons theory. For Hardin, there is no technical solution to the unrestricted open access to the commons: as more people pursue narrow economic self-interests, they put more stresses on the commons until its usefulness is depleted, greater management is imposed on it, or the land is portioned off into private property. No scientific or technological solution exists. Hardin's interpretation of the commons is an abstraction that is altogether alien to any iteration of the commons throughout history. Because the commons was simply a metaphor, his tragedy is a parable for the new language of Malthusian scarcity on a global scale, and there are no rules to shape its use.[4] Nevertheless, his essay sparked intense criticism of the idea of shared land use and revived a longstanding theoretical debate on the economics of the commons. In response to Hardin and other critics of the commons, economist and Nobel laureate Elinor Ostrom resuscitated the concept of the commons by expounding on the value and importance of common pool resources to past and future cultures.[5] At the heart of Ostrom's work is the notion that common-pool resources and the common good share an aversion to exclusion or privatization. They require cooperation, conversation, and the revival of community. For Ostrom, the future of success of the commons rests in the promotion of collective land-use that marries open dialog and participation, social and ecological responsibility, and a chastened appreciation of the current state of global environmental crisis. On this path, Wall and Ostrom see some hope in a more sustainable future.[6]

The history of the commons helps us to envision a more sustainable future on two counts. First, it allows us to analyze the success or failure of a property regime in practice rather than in theory. As Wall argues, "There is no value-free yardstick that can define the success or failure of commons."[7] Historical empiricism offers an effective lens for achieving greater clarity. Merging intellectual and material histories with one eye firmly on contemporary debate, Wall offers up an applied history that will serve students, scholars, policymakers, and activists. In addition, Wall leaves his readers with an important topic for further conversation. Although he concludes that the commons is an important and underused management tool that might sustainably alter how we exploit nature, he questions whether property-rights regimes can be steered effectively in this kind of direction. Good books spur provocative discourse, and Wall provides the context for a vital debate on how to engage the commons as a means of ensuring both social equity and environmental sustainability. Sustainability and the commons are linked by perceptions of time: the commons constitutes one of the oldest and most universal methods of land use, but sustainability looks forward over both short and long time frames. The history lesson of the much-maligned commons might help to encourage more forethought on long-term thinking.

Acknowledgments

The following individuals read drafts, made suggestions, and improved this book—Michel Bauwens, Emily Blyth, Martin Empson, Amanda Penfold, Andrea Claire Smith, Daniel Taghioff, and Dan Whittall. Thank you to James Sheils for preparing the index. The mistakes are all mine.

1

Commons Ecology

London and its environs would have no parks today if commoners had not asserted their rights, and as the nineteenth century drew on rights of recreation were more important than rights of pasture, and were defended vigilantly by the Commons Preservation Society. We owe to these premature "Greens" such urban lungs as we have. More than that, if it had not been for the stubborn defence by Newbury commoners of their rights to the Greenham Common, where on earth could NATO have parked its Nukes?[1]

The siege of Namur in 1695 is perhaps best known from Laurence Sterne's novel *Tristram Shandy*, but it is as good a place as any to start this discussion of the commons in history. In Sterne's novel, Tristram's Uncle Toby becomes obsessed with the siege where he received a mysterious groin injury. He builds a large-scale replica of the battle that he shows to his increasingly frustrated fiancée, Widow Wadham. The novel, filmed under the title *A Cock and Bull Story*, is known for its humor, brilliance, and somewhat insane plot developments, including the romance between the Widow Wadham and Uncle Toby. The real-life siege took place between British and French forces and led to an episode of commoning in Kirk Yetholm, a border town in the north of England, now in Scotland, that was famed for its association with gypsy travelers. During the siege of Namur, a gypsy by the name of Young saved the life of a Captain Bennet. In gratitude, the captain built cottages and leased them to Young and other gypsies. In addition, they and their descendants were given the right to cut turf and peat and graze cattle and horses on Yetholm Common.[2]

The story is traditional, and another version suggests that the gypsies were granted hospitality in 1745 after they rescued a horse that was owned by Sir William Bennet and stolen by Jacobites. Although the stories are disputed, there is no doubt that the travelers settled in the area and were granted common rights. Commoning in all its diversity includes collective ownership of land and other resources as well as the right of certain individuals to enjoy the property of others. The commons is a topic of increasing interest, and numerous studies link commons to environmental sustainability. The term has varied connotations—some negative (in terms of notions of the tragedy of the commons and associated mismanagement) and some positive or even poetic (as "a mythic landscape, a political metaphor, a utopian community").[3]

Overview

This book argues that property rights are essential to understanding sustainability. Property rights over land and other resources help condition how we interact with our wider environment. This book looks at a particular form of property ownership—the commons. Chapter 1 outlines different definitions of the commons, describes the tragedy of the commons, and discusses how different forms of common-pool property influence the environment. The environmental implications of commons within a historical context are illustrated with case studies from England, India, and Mongolia. Chapter 2 looks at the extent to which commons, where apparently sustainable, are maintained by cultural norms and not purely selfish economic considerations. Chapter 3 argues that the history of the commons is political. Rather than failing, many commons have been destroyed by invasion or eroded by the introduction of market economies. Their destruction has often led to environmental degradation. But commons are not (as some seem to suggest) a utopian alternative to systems based on private property. Their creation and maintenance has often involved conflict between individuals, social classes, communities, and even species. Chapter 4 discusses the kinds of questions we need to ask if we are to be good ancestors so that our activities do not threaten the future of our children and their children. The extent to which commons can be used to create a more sustainable future is the central theme of this chapter.

Commons, Sustainability, and Environmental History

Environmental history may help us make better decisions about how to move toward a more sustainable future. Today human society appears to be struggling to deal with sustainability, if *sustainability* is defined as the ability of present society to exist without damaging future generations. Climate change is already causing temperatures to rise, species are becoming extinct at an increasing rate, and other environmental problems seem set to multiply. Can history help us sustain history so that human beings can prosper without eroding the basic life-support systems for our species on this planet? Historical examples should not be used to advocate a return to some supposedly ideal state of nature. Rather than looking for a previous golden green age, the literary theorist Tim Morton has argued that we should be "nostalgic for the future, helping people figure out that the ecological 'paradise' has not occurred yet."[4] Although the creation of paradise may be a little ambitious, this short book suggests that the study of common-pool property rights can help us to develop a more sustainable future. Commons fit with Morton's notion of nostalgia for the future. They sometimes are seen as archaic institutions that can be traced to prehistoric times, but they can also be understood to include free software and cyberspace.

The link between environmental sustainability and commons has been discussed since at least the time of Aristotle in the fourth century BCE. In 1968, the biologist Garrett Hardin, in a paper on the tragedy of the commons that was published in the journal *Science*, made the case against commons. He argued that common ownership was a root cause of environmental degradation. In contrast, Elinor Ostrom, who won a Nobel Prize in economics for her work on commons, argued that under certain circumstances commons can be environmentally sustainable. Other thinkers see the commons as a solution to problems such as deforestation and climate change. The U.S. activist and writer Jay Walljasper has argued with polemical passion that rebuilding "the commons and defending the rights of Mother Earth are really the same cause."[5] Even more optimistically, Massimo De Angelis, a UK-based political economist, has stated, "My interest in the commons is grounded in a desire for the conditions necessary to promote social justice, sustainability, and happy lives for all. As simple as that."[6] However, the commons debate is far from simple. Detailed and complex discussions thick with epistemological and ontological nuances have ranged across several disciplines, including anthropology, ecology, legal theory, and economics. Even the term *commons* has been debated and argued over at some length.

What Is the Commons?

Property rights determine access to resources(including natural resources such as forests and fields) and therefore condition how we look after them or fail to do so. As such, property rights influence environmental sustainability. The phrase *property rights* is, like most terms used by social scientists, subject to debate and disagreement. Jeremy Waldron, a professor of law and philosophy from New Zealand, has provided a simple working definition—"the concept of a system of rules governing access to and control of material resources."[7] Property rights establish relationships between people and things. They are also social and shape relationships between different groups of people. Property rights determine who gets what and who is excluded in terms of access to resources. Understanding how property rights have changed is vital in helping us to understand not just environmental history but history in general. Changes in ownership are often matched by deep changes in how we live and in the nature of our society. It has been suggest that the "history of property relations in a given society is thus, in a way, the history of the society itself."[8]

As individuals, we may own land, personal possessions, or shares in a company. The state may own military aircraft, civil service paper clips, and roads. The idea that a community can own property collectively is often forgotten, and the allied notion that individuals may have access to the property of others by right rather than as theft may also seem unusual. However, various forms of communal ownership have been widespread in the past. The Romans, for example, recognized several different kinds of collective property in their legal system.

Elinor Ostrom makes a distinction between common-pool property and common-pool resources. She argues that commons emerged because private ownership may be impractical in some circumstances, but her starting point was the existence of common resources. Ostrom suggests that it is difficult to exclude people from a common-pool resource, which leads to overuse and potentially to degradation and destruction. She felt that a fishing ground is a good example because it is difficult to prevent people from entering and catching as many fish as they like. If too many fish are caught, they might disappear entirely, leading to the mutual destruction of both fish and the

fishing economy. Common-pool resources are a problem because they can be overexploited, and Ostrom spent a lifetime
trying to solve this problem.[9]

A common-pool resource is not the same as common property. Common-pool property is not a resource but a form of
ownership. Commons can be seen as a particular category of
property rights based on collective rather than state or private
ownership, although there is some overlap between these three
categories. Commons can be unowned and accessed by all or
owned by a community and managed collectively. Property can
also be owned by an individual or institution but may be open
to others to use under certain conditions. Thus, commons may
even be privately owned but open to use by commoners. For
example, in England and Wales there are currently 500,000
hectares of common land that are owned privately but with
access for all.[10] Many of the world's fisheries and forests are
both common-pool resources and managed via common-pool
property systems. In recent decades, there has been explosive
growth in cybercommons in the form of the World Wide Web,
free software, and other virtual property:

The legal theorist Yochai Benkler has contrasted common pool property with private property in the following way. "Property" (by which
he means private property) puts one person in control of how a resource is used; in contrast, no single individual controls how a commons is used. To a greater or lesser extent, a commons is a shared
resource.[11]

Benkler argues that commons can be divided into different
types according to two distinct parameters. The first parameter is whether they are open to everyone (for example, the
atmosphere is an open commons). He also notes the existence
of "limited-access common resources" where ownership is collective but limited to a group of villagers or members of an
association. Common land and irrigation systems are examples
of such managed commons.[12] Benkler's second parameter is

whether commons are regulated or unregulated—that is, are rules of use and access agreed to and enforced? Although Garrett Hardin suggests in his "Tragedy" paper that unregulated commons lead to environmental degradation via overexploitation, Elinor Ostrom argues that communities can often find ways of regulating commons to solve this potential problem.

The notion of *usufruct* is essential to the regulation of both common-pool property and common-pool resources. The term, derived from Roman law, denotes the right to use and benefit from property that belongs to someone else, as long as the property is not damaged. A Roman tenant could enjoy the fruits of land or other forms of property that were owned by a landlord, as long as the property was maintained appropriately. Roman legal theorists debated usufruct rules at length, as is indicated by accounts of the rights of the "usufructuary" to "enjoy" a property while not owning it. William Alexander Hunter, a Scottish jurist and politician, notes that according to Roman law a usufructuary was not allowed to cut down fruit trees but could take their branches to use as stakes for growing vines. Dead trees could be chopped up for firewood, and the usufructuary could dig lime or gravel for repairing his property. Hunter noted that bees "on the land belong to the usufructuary; and he has the right of fishing, fowling, and hunting."[13]

The word *usufruct* is derived from the Latin phrase *usus et fructus*, which means "use and enjoyment of fruits." The concept of usufruct extends beyond the rights of ancient Roman tenants. It has an obvious connection with sustainability in establishing an appropriate use of property so that it can be enjoyed by future generations. Karl Marx, writing in *Das Kapital,* explains this principle:

From the standpoint of a higher economic form of society, private ownership of the globe by single individuals will appear quite absurd as private ownership of one man by another. Even a whole society, a nation, or even all simultaneously existing societies taken together, are not the owners of the globe. They are only its possessors, its usu-fructuries, and like *boni patres familias*, they must hand it down to succeeding generations in an improved condition.[14]

Usufruct rights might vary widely. In medieval Britain, common land was owned by the local manor within a feudal system, but commoners had a range of usage rights. Pasture rights allowed them to graze animals. Pannage was the right to allow pigs to forage for acorns and beech mast. The right to take bracken for animal bedding was also covered by estover. Turbary was the right to dig peat or turf, which provided fuel in medieval England. Piscary was the right to catch fish, and commons in the soil meant that sand, gravel, or stone could be taken for building or mending paths.[15] The term *estover* is de-rived from the Latin phrase *est opus*, which means "it is neces-sary." The 1720 English document *The Law of Commons and Commoners* explains this notion, noting that tenants required access to resources so they could sustain themselves, pay rent, and perform other services.[16] They needed to graze cattle, and it was necessary for them to have access to fallen wood to make their fires. The economy functioned by allowing commoners to sustain themselves so they could provide landowners with la-bor, commodities, or in later times cash payments. For over a thousand years in Germany, heathland provided common land for estover, where commoners grazed their animals, gathered firewood, picked berries and mushrooms, and even kept bee-hives.[17] The concept of estover suggests that property rights can be more flexible and varied than we often understand in a society where much property is private and individualized.

According to the legal theorist Carol M. Rose, Roman law also recognized a range of forms of property.[18] *Res publicae* included property such as a public park or navigable river that was owned by the state but open to the community. *Res com-munis* included light and air, which could not be owned by particular groups or individuals and were enjoyed by all. *Res nullius* included objects that were unowned because they were wild or abandoned, such as stray dogs or lions. *Res privatae* included property owned by individuals, while *res divini juris* included possessions that belonged to the gods, such as temples. European and U.S. law are based on Roman law, but in recent centuries, such a flexible approach to property has been generally overlooked.

There are many other historical examples of usufruct, estover, and communal property rights. Joel Kovel, an ecosocialist activist and writer, notes that although usufruct is a Latin term taken from Roman law, its roots can be found in Babylon's Code of Hammurabi from 1750 BCE, as well as Islamic and Aztec law.[19] Legal theorists and historians have become increasingly aware that prior to the period of European colonialism, commons were the rule rather than the exception across much of our planet. The jurist Sir Henry Maine in his book *Ancient Law*, first published in 1861, argues that in the past property was at first originally communal in nature rather than individually owned.[20]

In his book *Changes in the Land*, the environmental historian William Cronon shows how changing patterns of ownership transformed the ecology of New England between 1600 and 1800.[21] The concept of buying and selling land was alien to the indigenous people, but granting usufruct rights or exchanging such rights was possible. Similar attitudes to land were apparently universal in the Americas prior to colonialism. In Australia, which was dominated by indigenous commons, notions of private ownership of land were unknown to the population before the arrival of the British. The existence of common community ownership was also important in India and, despite considerable enclosure, remains so in the twenty-first century.[22] There are numerous examples of commons from continental Europe.[23] With the erosion of indigenous control in North America, colonialists created new commons, although these too have diminished over the last two hundred years. Commons are still significant in Mongolia to this day.[24] Commons can be found in the Middle East. The anthropologist Dawn Chatty examined the Badia, a system of commons management extending over much of Syria.[25] Examples of historical and modern commons can be found on virtually every part of the planet.

Contested Commons

Commons have been examined from a wide variety of perspectives. Historians, social movement researchers, anthropologists, geographers, and legal theorists have investigated commons. Marxists have advocated commons as a form of communism, and some libertarians who are critical of socialism have also embraced the concept of commons and alternative forms of property rights.

Legal approaches to commons are well known, from land and other traditional commons to the new commons of software and the World Wide Web.[26] The *Cornell Law Journal*, for example, devoted a special issue to the discussion of information commons. Commons have been sustained using customary law, which includes often unwritten traditions created through long practice, although formal written law has often displaced this system. The legal pluralist approach stresses that alternative legal systems may overlap and that formal law should not ignore the existence of alternative systems of governance. Legal pluralism has been especially important in former colonial states, where traditional non-Western forms of law are beginning to be recognized again. The 1992 Mabo ruling in Australia gave force to customary law and traditional forms of community land ownership after a challenge was mounted by the Torres Straits people for recognition of their land rights. The Mabo case overruled the legal fiction that Australia was *terra nullius* (an empty land) before the arrival of the British. In Canada, the *Delgamuukw v. British Columbia* (1997) case had a similar effect. Christopher Rodgers, Margherita Pieraccini, Eleanor A. Straughton, and Angus Winchester have studied the environmental history of the commons in Britain using the legal pluralist perspective, suggesting that both formal law and traditions of customary law help to explain how commons work.[27]

A useful collection of essays titled *Contested Commons: Conversations between Economists and Anthropologists* seeks to create a conversation between researchers who study commons.[28] It argues that the research assumptions of the two disciplines lead to different ways of understanding commons. Briefly, economists are seen as stressing outcomes, and anthropologists processes. Anthropologists see power issues as strongly influencing research, while economists view researchers as neutral. Economists prefer pared-down models of explanation, which are as simple as possible, whereas anthropologists seek "thick descriptions" that are richly complex and subtle. Although historical approaches to commons are likely to be closer to anthropology than economics, environmental historians may not always be as explicit in examining their overall theoretical framework to research as anthropologists are. However, some anthropological approaches may be so detailed and localized that they may be less useful for informing approaches to a sustainable future, and theoretical nuances may overwhelm empirical observation. The appropriate balance between detailed local research and broad historical sweep creates a dilemma that is difficult to resolve. Anthropologists remind us that commons may be very diverse and that evidence gathered from one case-study example may not be generalizable to other contexts.

Different schools of political thought have also taken a keen interest in the commons. Liberalism is associated with individualism and private property rather than collectivism and communal property, but some liberal thinkers have embraced the commons. Elinor Ostrom's work was influenced, perhaps surprisingly, by liberal theorists rather than collectivist socialists. These included Alexis de Tocqueville, the nineteenth-century French political thinker and author *Democracy in America*, and the Austrian economist Friedrich Hayek. De Tocqueville contrasts locally developed associations and the direct democracy of New England town meetings with those of a centralized state, arguing that the emerging American democracy was based on self-government and self-organization. Elinor and her husband, Vincent, celebrated democracy as self-organized and participatory, which fueled their interest in the commons. In 2012, just before her death, Elinor Ostrom delivered the annual Hayek lecture to the free-market think tank the Institute of Economic Affairs (IEA) in London. The IEA, which has done much to promote her work on the commons, argues that she showed that environmental problems could be tackled by local people without the need for strong government intervention. *Wikipedia* and a range of other new cybercommons have been strongly supported by libertarians, who see them as a force promoting personal freedom. Indeed, *Wikipedia* cofounder Jimmy Wales is an objectivist who follows the philosophy of the libertarian thinker Ayn Rand. He also cites, like Ostrom, the influence of Friedrich Hayek's essay "The Use of Knowledge in Society" on his thinking.[29] Hayek argues that knowledge is dispersed through society and that therefore governments are often unlikely to be informed enough to make good decisions. In contrast, a free market provides a more effective way of making use of dispersed knowledge than central action by government. Jimmy Wales was inspired by this insight in creating an encyclopedia that relies on millions of participants rather than a small number of supposed experts.

Many on the left also have advocated the commons. Karl Marx and his coauthor Friedrich Engels were fascinated by the "communistic" property rights of peasants and saw the enclosure and subsequent destruction of the commons as a key stage in the creation of a market-based social system. Marx's interest in the commons is a thread that ran through his entire life's work. One of his earliest pieces of journalism looks at the fight by peasants to continue to gather fallen wood in German forest commons.[30] Engels argues that Marx became a socialist partly because of this attack on the rights of the commoners to pick up branches for their fires as they had done for many centuries. In his most important work, *Das Kapital*, Marx describes how commons were enclosed in England and Scotland. Marx also worked on his anthropological notes in the last years before he died, and his study of commons was a central part of this quest to understand both earlier societies and existing indigenous groups.[31] Engels discusses the indigenous North American commons in his work and wrote a history of the commons in Germany.[32] Both Marx and Engels were fascinated by the anthropologist Lewis Morgan's book *Ancient Society*, which was based partly on Morgan's research into the Haudenosaunee or Iroquois confederation. They also note that the Roman author Tacitus believed that the early German tribes held land and property as commons.

Although Marxists have generally been less interested in the commons than Marx or Engels were, there are some important exceptions. The school of British Marxist historians that includes E. P. Thompson and Christopher Hill examined commons in some detail. Edward Palmer Thompson, usually referred to as E. P. Thompson, is probably the most important historian to have studied the environmental effects of commons. A lifelong Marxist, he fought the Nazis in Italy during World War II as a member of a tank unit. He joined the Communist Party but left in disgust after the Soviet invasion of Hungary in 1956. He was interested in promoting a democratic, environmentally friendly, and open politics in opposition to Stalinism.

Highly politically active, he became an important campaigner for nuclear disarmament during the 1980s. Before his death in 1993, he wrote a series of important books, including *The Making of the English Working Class* and works on the poet William Blake and the Victorian designer, artist, writer, socialist leader, and environmentalist William Morris.

Thompson's essay "Custom, Law and Common Right" is a detailed account of the changing nature of commons in England. He argues that commons have evolved as a result of battles over access between owners and users, with local elites trying to restrict access to commons and resistance from commoners spanning many centuries.[33] He notes, for example, that successful opposition to enclosure during the nineteenth century led to the conservation of much green space, including the creation of many public parks. London's Hyde Park and Hampstead Heath exist because of protests to prevent the enclosure of commons. Thompson's work is distinctly Marxist in that it stresses the role of social class and class conflict, yet he avoids economic reductionism, arguing that cultural factors cannot be reduced to some supposed superstructure. Thompson uses detailed historical work to show how commons, far from being static, varied from one location to another because of specific local customs and clashes: "there cannot be a forest or a chase in the country which did not have some dramatic episode of conflict over common right in the eighteenth century."[34] Rabbit warrens placed on commons led commoners to riot and dig them up in many cases because they damaged their crops. Thompson notes, for example, that in 1749 commoners (including local coal miners) converged on a warrener in the Charnwood Forest of Leicestershire. In the battle, one commoner was killed, and troops were brought in, but as a result a right "of common was proved for twenty-six neighboring towns and villages, and Charnwood Forest remained unenclosed for a further half-century."[35] Thompson's book

Whigs and Hunters looks at battles between commoners and landowners in eighteenth-century Berkshire and Hampshire in England. At the time of his death in 1993, he was working on a study of indigenous commons in North America.

Christopher Hill, born in 1912, was radicalized partly by a holiday trip to 1930s Germany that awakened him to the horrors of Nazi Germany. Like his colleague Thompson, he joined the Communist Party, fought in World War II, and left the Communists in disgust after the invasion of Hungary in 1957. He was a founding social historian who believed that history had to take account of individual personal experience. His work showed how conflict between different social classes—such as the conflict between Parliamentarian and Royalist forces during the English Civil War in the seventeenth century—centered on disputes over property rights, including the commons. He researched the case of the Diggers (also known as the "true Levellers"), who occupied St. Georges Hill in Surrey and attempted to live communally on the commons.[36]

The autonomist Marxist, Peter Linebaugh, a student of E.P. Thompson during the 1970s, drew on Thompson's work and has written a number of important books on the commons. Autonomism is close to anarchism in that it rejects the state and political parties; it stresses the creative nature of human beings to make history. With Marcus Rediker, Linebaugh coauthored *The Many-Headed Hydra: Sailors, Slaves, Commoners and the Hidden History of the Revolutionary Atlantic* and examined the environmental and social nature of the commons in *The Magna Carta Manifesto: Liberties and Commons for All*.[37] Massimo De Angelis, an autonomist and political economist at the University of East London, has argued that commons have to be actively constructed. He has noted that common-pool property, an active community, and communing are all necessary to create a working commons.[38] Titles such as *Empire*[39] and *Commonwealth*[40] by the Italian political philosopher

Antonio Negri and U.S. literary theorist Michael Hardt have also discussed the potential for common-pool property, both in cyberspace and physical forms.

Another autonomist, the philosopher George Caffentzis, has argued that common-pool property is an important aspect of Islamic economics, noting that the Koran states that the "people are partners in three things: water, pastures and fire." Early Islamic societies shared the proceeds of mining among community members, and examples of community ownership of land and other resources were widespread.[41] Caffentzis also argues that, in his view, there are two broad approaches to the study of commons. One approach, from a social movement perspective, is opposed to capitalism and sees the defense and extension of commons as an alternative to market relations. The other approach ignores the existence of capitalism as a social and economic system but understands commons as complementary to a wider market-based economy. He conceptualizes the world of Elinor Ostrom and allied researchers as coming into this second category. He described Ostrom as a "Neo-Hardinian."[42] Although this description might seem problematic, given Ostrom's work (which challenges Hardin's "tragedy of the commons" thesis), a distinction can be seen between politically inspired and less overtly political approaches to the commons.

Thus, academics studying the commons can be split between those who broadly believe that commons are a problem (Garrett Hardin) and those who see them as potentially beneficial (Elinor Ostrom). Economists stress the material costs and benefits of commons, while anthropologists are more likely to highlight the cultural dimension. There also are revolutionary advocates of commons who literally champion a communistic and collectivist society and whose approach can be distinguished from researchers who are more modest in their assessment and less explicitly political.

Any study of the commons should be based on an awareness of such distinctions, but these different perspectives overlap. For example, all of these approaches emphasize the functional value of commons for maintaining environmental quality. All note the power dimension, but Marxists stress the role of conflict most strongly. Economists studying the commons are less focused on the effect of external conflict on them; however, it would be inaccurate to claim they ignore power relations in their entirety. Although Marxian approaches note the existence of a macro context of power relations and economic change at a social or even global level, other commons researchers are more focused on a micro context that examines why individual commons regimes may or may not conserve resources. Legal pluralist approaches to commons in drawing on traditional legal systems are linked to anthropology.

Like Elinor Ostrom, E. P. Thompson and the autonomists have shown a concern with the environmental effects of property rights and suggest that commons can be part of a more sustainable system. The ecosocialist economist Paul Burkett argues in *Ecological Economics and Marxism* that a communist society should be based on the ecological commons.[43] The political activist and social scientist Joel Kovel in his book *The Enemy of Nature: The End of Capitalism or the End of the World?* also notes the importance of commons as a source of a socially just and ecological society.[44]

Some libertarians argue that common-pool property rights may provide a way of solving environmental problems without extending the power of the state. Until recently, however, the most commonly heard argument is that commons are a source of environmental destruction rather than a solution to it, so it is important to outline the "tragedy of the commons" thesis before examining the concept of the ecological commons in more detail.

The Tragedy of the Commons

Garrett Hardin's article "The Tragedy of the Commons," published in the journal *Science* in 1968, puts forward the view that commons are a cause of environmental degradation. Unowned resources are unprotected and open to overexploitation. Hardin takes the hypothetical example of fields used for cattle grazing:

The tragedy of the commons develops in this way. Picture a pasture open to all. It is to be expected that each herdsman will try to keep as many cattle as possible on the commons. Such an arrangement may work reasonably satisfactorily for centuries because tribal wars, poaching, and disease keep the numbers of both man and beast well below the carrying capacity of the land. Finally, however, comes the day of reckoning, that is, the day when the long-desired goal of social stability becomes a reality. At this point, the inherent logic of the commons remorselessly generates tragedy.

As a rational being, each herdsman seeks to maximize his gain. Explicitly or implicitly, more or less consciously, he asks, "What is the utility to me of adding one more animal to my herd?" This utility has one negative and one positive component.

1. The positive component is a function of the increment of one animal. Since the herdsman receives all the proceeds from the sale of the additional animal, the positive utility is nearly + 1.
2. The negative component is a function of the additional overgrazing created by one more animal. Since, however, the effects of overgrazing are shared by all the herdsmen, the negative utility for any particular decision making herdsman is only a fraction of –1.

Adding together the component partial utilities, the rational herdsman concludes that the only sensible course for him to pursue is to add another animal to his herd. And another; and another. . . . But this is the conclusion reached by each and every rational herdsman sharing a commons. Therein is the tragedy. Each man is locked into a system that compels him to increase his herd without limit—in a world that is limited. Ruin is the destination toward which all men rush, each pursuing his own best interest in a society that believes in the freedom of the commons. Freedom in a commons brings ruin to all.[45]

Freedom will lead to disaster because of the free-rider problem—that is, if one user tries to conserve the commons by exploiting it less, other users will exploit it more. Thus, there is no incentive to conserve, and the commons will eventually be destroyed. According to Hardin, neither ecological sustainability nor prosperous development is possible in a commons; therefore, commons must be enclosed and either privatized or given to the state. Hardin's article gained huge attention and was cited by a wide variety of academics, including electrical engineers in journals such as *Systems Methods* and *Spectroscopy*; biologists in publications such as the *Journal of Forestry*, *Bioscience*, and *the Australian Medical Journal*; and social scientists in the *Journal of Applied Psychology*, *Current Anthropology*, and the *Journal of Conflict Resolution*.[46] Hardin's paper shaped how commons were perceived until Elinor Ostrom's Nobel Prize win challenged such pessimism. For most of us, because of Hardin, commons almost automatically mean tragedy.

The "tragedy of the commons" thesis is based on a long tradition that sees unowned property as a source of environmental degradation. The ancient Greek philosopher Aristotle notes that what is "common to the greatest number gets the least amount of care," suggesting that individuals pay most attention to what they own privately.[47] The nineteenth-century writer William Forster Lloyd asks skeptically, "Why are the cattle on a common so puny and stunted? Why is the common itself so bare-worn, and cropped so differently from the adjoining inclosures?"[48] The Austrian economist Ludwig von Mises notes that if "land is not owned by anybody, although legal formalism may call it public property, it is used without any regard to the disadvantages resulting." Von Mises observes that commoners do not care about "erosion of the soil, depletion of the exhaustible resources"; for them, "other impairments of the future utilization are external costs not entering into their calculation of input and output." Like Hardin, he argues that the commoner would "cut down trees without any regard for fresh shoots or reforestation."[49] Much conservation policy has been inspired by such assumptions. The anthropologist Dawn Chatty, writing about Syria, has argued that the nomadic Bedouins who lacked fixed boundaries were seen as overexploiting both domestic and wild animals in the region. Conservationists have argued that to preserve the Syrian environment, private property with clear borders was needed.[50] In his book *The Land Grabbers*, the British science journalist Fred Pearce argues that because of Hardin's argument that commons lead to disaster, millions of acres of land are threatened with seizure from nomadic pastoralists in countries as diverse as Kenya, Mozambique, and Jordan.[51]

The case against the commons is apparently overwhelming, yet rather than seeing commons as a cause of degradation, others have argued that they can be a sustainable solution to environmental problems. The best-known champion of the commons is Elinor Ostrom, to whose ideas we now turn.

Commons as a Solution

In 2009, Elinor Ostrom became the first and to date only woman to win a Nobel Prize for economics, strictly speaking the Sveriges Riksbank Prize in Economic Sciences, which she shared with Oliver Williamson. She was awarded the prize for her work on the commons. Elinor was a fascinating thinker and an unusual individual. Born in Los Angeles in 1933, she became interested in politics when she was encouraged to join a school debating society to reduce her stutter. She studied politics at university and enjoyed economics courses, but she had a fight on her hands because women were often discouraged in the 1960s from taking academic courses. Her PhD in political economy examined the management of water resources in California, which she later realized were commons.[52] With her husband, Vincent Ostrom, she looked at how people might work to conserve their local environments. Her key concerns— such as sustainability, defense of indigenous peoples, social equality, and grassroots democracy—may suggest that she was a radical leftist, yet her intellectual influences included market liberals such as Hayek and Tocqueville.

Elinor Ostrom examined hundreds of case study examples of commons across the world. She claims that the tragedy of what might be termed the *unmanaged commons* is the real target of Garrett Hardin's criticism. She suggests that state control or privatization of commons might also fail and that commoners could manage commons adequately in some circumstances:

> Some scholarly articles about the "tragedy of the commons" recommend that "the state" control most natural resources to prevent their destruction; others recommend that privatizing those resources will resolve the problem. What one can observe in the world, however, is that neither the state nor market is uniformly successful in enabling individuals to sustain long-term, productive use of natural resource systems. Further, communities of individuals have relied on institutions resembling neither the state nor the market to govern some resource systems with reasonable degrees of success over periods of time.[53]

For Ostrom, although three theoretical models—the "tragedy of the commons," the prisoners' dilemma, and political scientist Mancur Olson's model of collective action—suggest pessimistically that it is difficult for individuals to come together to solve collective problems, in practice there are some grounds for optimism. The prisoners' dilemma is a model used by game theorists to suggest that self-interest may prevent cooperative behavior. In the model, two suspected criminals are arrested and held in separate cells, and each is told that if he or she confesses, then he or she will receive a reduced sentence. If neither confesses, they both will go free, but their mutual suspicion tends to lead them to confess because they do not trust the other not to confess. Thus, self-interest leads to a worse outcome for both because by confessing they go to prison rather than being freed due to lack of evidence. With similar effect, Mancur Olson argues that it is unlikely that individuals will act collectively, action is costly and inconvenient, and therefore it is better to do nothing and "free ride" on the action of others.[54] Because each individual waits for others to act, ultimately none act, and collective problems are left unsolved. Each model suggests that collective action is likely to be impossible and that individual solutions to problems are the best that can be achieved.

Elinor Ostrom did not reject these models completely, but she believed that the free-rider problem that they indicated, where self-interest leads to collective disaster, can often be overcome. Ostrom placed ecological sustainability at the heart of her work, arguing that to maintain prosperity individuals must be able to sustain their local environments. She argued that although centralized solutions imposed by governments can sometimes be effective, decentralized local control of the environment is often likely to be successful. This is because local communities are more likely to develop trust between individuals and because environmental knowledge requires detailed local knowledge that distant bureaucrats may lack.

Since Ostrom won her Nobel Prize, the popularity of the notion of commons as at least a partial solution to environmental degradation has grown. Fittingly, she and her husband, Vincent, created an open-source library of papers, books, and articles on commons research that is available at http://dlc.dlib.indiana .edu/dlc. She also recycled her Nobel Prize money into further research into sustainability and property rights. Although not a historian, Elinor Ostrom argues that a historical perspective is vital if we are to understand why and how commons may work to sustain environmental quality. When she died of pancreatic cancer in June 2012, the *Economist* magazine in its obituary provided a useful summary of her approach:

It seemed to Elinor Ostrom that the world contained a large body of common sense. People, left to themselves, would sort out rational ways of surviving and getting along. Although the world's arable land, forests, fresh water and fisheries were all finite, it was possible to share them without depleting them and to care for them without fighting. While others wrote gloomily of the tragedy of the commons, seeing only overfishing and overfarming in a free-for-all of greed, Mrs. Ostrom, with her loud laugh and louder tops, cut a cheery and contrarian figure.[55]

Commons History: England, Mongolia, and India

Commons have often been seen as empty, unowned, unimportant, and irrelevant. The Australian constitution claimed that the country was an empty land before the arrival of Europeans. The idea that Australia was inhabited and that the land was governed according to complex property rights that maintained environmental quality was ignored for centuries. The work of Elinor Ostrom, E. P. Thompson, Yochai Benkler, and other thinkers who have studied common-pool resources and property has made a difference. Rather than being seen as nonplaces, commons are now considered to be worthy of study and increasingly are seen as important. Although long-term studies of commons over many centuries are still relatively rare, detailed accounts of commons show both shared and divergent features. This section outlines histories of commons in Mongolia, England, and India, three parts of the world where historical records illustrate how functioning commons have changed over time.

Commons are often very diverse. As the development economist Robert Wade showed in *Village Republics: Economic Conditions for Collective Action in South India*, his study of communal management of land and irrigation in Southern India, the organization of commons may vary greatly from one village to the next.[56] Yet even across continents, the history of commons shows some features of parallel development. Most of the relatively good accounts of the historical commons in England examine enclosure, particularly between the sixteenth and eighteenth centuries, but a number of studies summarize a much longer period of change. The Open Spaces Society, founded in 1865 as the Commons Preservation Society, published a booklet that outlines commons history from prehistory to the twenty-first century.[57] As noted previously, E. P. Thompson and Christopher Rodgers and his colleagues, among others, have also undertaken detailed research into the English and Welsh commons. There are several good historical studies of commons in India, including economist Minoti Chakravarty-Kaul's work on the Punjab[58] and Madhav Gadgil and Ramachandra Guha's ecological history of the country.[59] Mongolia, where commons are still extremely important, provides a contrast with England and India. There are a number of studies of Mongolian commons over many centuries.

In all three areas, it seems that commons existed prior to written records. In England, medieval systems of land tenure incorporated features of much earlier forms of collective ownership. Records show that an open-field system of commons existed in the seventh century and, as has been noted, that Roman Britain saw the use of usufruct rights that gave access to land along with varied notions of common property rights. The pre-Roman Iron Age societies seem to have practiced communal land ownership that may have shared features with the Irish Brehon system that derives from prehistoric roots. The archeologist Susan Oothuizen has suggested that archeological evidence indicates that commons created in prehistory may have influenced land-use patterns into the Anglo-Saxon period.[60] Kate Ashbrook and Nicola Hodgson from the Open Spaces Society note that place names provide evidence of early commons: for example, "Somerset" means "land of the summer dwellers," people who occupied the lowland moors and marshes for summer grazing only.[61]

North Meadow, Cricklade, in the county of Wiltshire, illustrates both the environmental richness of English commons at their best and their ancient nature. According to the conservation body English Nature, North Meadow has been traditionally managed for over a thousand years and is one of the most important wildflower locations in the United Kingdom. Over two hundred fifty significant plant species can be found on the meadow, "including abundant grasses such as red fescue *Festucarubra*, perennial rye-grass *Loliumperenne*, meadow foxtail *Alopecuruspratensis*, crested dog's tail *Cynosuruscristatus* and yellow oatgrass *Trisetum flavescens*."[62] About 80 percent of the rare snakeshead fritillary *Fritillaria meleagri* in Britain are found on North Meadow. The meadow floods in winter, the waters giving rise to the rich habitat. The meadow has been commons since at least the Anglo-Saxon period. A court leet, which is still made up of democratically chosen commoners, regulates the meadow. On Lammas Day, August 1, the meadow is opened up to the commoners' cattle to graze until February. Leet courts were used to maintain manorial commons across England and can be traced back to the Anglo-Saxon period. Lammas Day, which is important in the calendar of many English commons, hints at a Roman or pre-Roman origin for such practices, as it marks the prehistoric Celtic festival of Lughnasadh. Common land, which can be used for a period of months communally after August 1, is often found in England and Wales and is known as Lammas land. Fields that had been used to grow wheat or other cereals were opened to grazing animals after the summer harvest.[63]

In England, truly communal property that was owned by the community seems to have been brought under the control of local landowners within a manorial system during the Anglo-Saxon period. After 1066, a feudal society saw land vested in the ownership of the monarch and controlled by the Norman aristocracy. On a local basis, land continued to be administered by the manor. Manorial courts recognized customary law and granted a variety of common rights to serfs, including land use and the rights to gather fallen branches and other resources from woodland. Land used directly for the benefit of the lord was known as the *demesne*. Open fields were divided into strips for the use of the serfs. Although these often were challenged as inefficient, the economist Donald McCloskey argues that they were a way that serfs could spread risk. Different strips of land had different microclimates and were a hedge against problems of crop failure due to changing weather patterns and pests.[64] *Waste* was the term used to describe unenclosed land where peasants could graze animals and gather wood beyond the open fields and demesne.

A process of formalization, where unwritten customary rights were recorded and boundaries created, ensued gradually over many centuries. The 1236 Statute of Merton recognized private ownership of land by the local manor as well as the rights of the population to access to land and usufruct rights. It also established coppice woodlands. Coppicing allows the growth of staves of wood used for thatching, tool making, and construction. At the time, woods were removed to make way for more grazing.[65] The lord could bring land into assart, which meant transferring it from commons to personal use, but he had to leave sufficient land for serfs.

Management of the commons included detailed measures to prevent disease and to deal with the conflicting rights and interests of different commoners. Christopher Rodgers and his colleagues note practices (such as the exclusion of infectious cattle and the ringing of pigs to prevent them from grubbing up common land) and rules (dealing with matters such as the behavior of rams and the number of cattle that could be placed on the commons by an individual) that relate to commons. These rules were common in different locations and were similar to practices in Scandinavia, so they may be derived from a wider and older folk culture, brought perhaps into northern England by the Vikings:

Intercommoning, where different communities shared the use of the land, may have originated in nomadic grazing practice but was gradually restricted and removed. "Stinting" that rationed the use of the commons also became more common after the fourteenth century. [A] . . . gradual erosion of commons rights occurred from the sixteenth century. . . . By the nineteenth century, commons were drastically reduced and their use had been largely transformed. In England, at present, commons on the higher moorlands are still important for grazing and lowland commons are used chiefly for leisure pursuits such as dog walking and kite flying.[66]

Bonnie McCay and Alyne Delaney, participants in an international academic conference on the commons, visited Cleeve Common in Gloucestershire in 2008. Their account shows some of these features of English commons and illustrates that commons generally have a history and are rooted in specific localities:

we hired a car and drove on narrow winding roads in search of "Cleeve Common," a large limestone grassland northeast of the town of Cheltenham, high on a hill overlooking the enclosed fields and towns of this lush part of the Cotswolds. After a couple of wrong turns and stops to take pictures, we made it, our first visit to a classic agrarian common-land, English style. We saw the list of rules and regulations—"the commons" are indeed regulated!—opened the gate—yes, they are fenced—, and were amazed to watch para-gliders playing the winds among the cattle grazing on this hilltop common, a reminder of the importance of common-lands for multiple uses and also their adaptability to changing tastes and values! It was also an eye-opener to learn that in England such common-lands are not public lands, but rather are privately held lands—this one by the descendants of the Lords of the Manor of Southam and Bishops Cleeve—to which neighboring people, usually farmers, hold common use rights. That fact reflected the broader message of the many papers given at the Cheltenham meeting of IASC: a reminder of the variety and historical/cultural specificity of "the commons." The web-site for the Conservators of Cleeve Commons (yes, there are people organized to take care of it) describes the landscape as a "natural limestone grasslands," but the deeper history of the place includes its having been cleared about 10,000 years ago—a reminder of how much what we see and cherish as "natural" can just as well be seen and cherished as created through interactions with people.[67]

In Mongolia, far from England, some similar features of change and development are apparent. In the early medieval period, nomadic herders traveled across huge territories with little or no interference. Access to land over time remained communal but also became more formalized and restricted. Genghis Khan (1162?–1227) granted land to his allies to reinforce his political authority and military power. The Mongolian nobility gained formal control of communal pastureland and were able to tax herders. Thus, formal boundaries were established, apparently for the first time. As in England, an essentially feudal system was introduced, with a monarch who granted land to an elite, whose members were rewarded for their loyalty and extracted wealth from the wider population. The reintroduction of Buddhism in 1586 was another important development. As with Britain's churches, in this case Buddhist monasteries were a major owner of land and an important political and economic power. The formalization of land rights under the Buddhist authority and the system of patronage established by Genghis Khan developed further with the Manchu Qing dynasty occupation in 1691. The Chinese occupiers drew up a legal code and divided the land, eventually creating a hundred military territories known as *khoshuun.*[68] Herders who previously moved from one territory to another had to remain within the jurisdiction where they were born, showing allegiance to the ruler of such territory.[69]

After Manchu rule ended, more formal structures remained, but transhumance with herders moving their animals seasonally was maintained as long as herders remained in the same *khoshuun.* Gradually, some privately control campsites emerged, but communal and nomadic ways of life continued. The creation of a twentieth-century Mongolian Republic, at least briefly, led to a return to more flexible and locally controlled property ownership. In 1925, feudal and religious structures were abolished. In the twentieth century, the Soviet Union introduced collectivism, which peaked in 1959 with 99 percent of herders cemented into this system of state central control of agriculture. With the collapse of the Soviet Union, a market-oriented Mongolian Republic emerged that saw attempts to privatize land holdings. In the twenty-first century, a greater understanding of the benefits of communal herding may be reemerging. With economic and political changes, communing has diminished. Although commons still exist and nomadic herding continues, the territory used by herders has shrunk, their control over their animals has fallen, and informal regulation has been increasingly replaced by formal controls. Patterns of land use have become less flexible over time.[70] Yet the commons remains in the twenty-first century.

Mongolia shows also that commons may be difficult to eliminate or control centrally but are influenced by political events and socioeconomic change. Genghis Khan, Tibetan Buddhism, Chinese invasion, the Soviet experience, and market-based policies encouraged by external bodies such as the World Bank have all shaped the commons. Nonetheless, despite formalization and erosion, the Mongolian pastoral commons remains. The anthropologist David Sneath has highlighted the libertarian nature of Mongolian society, arguing that central control has remained relatively weak and that herders have enjoyed a large measure of independence throughout many centuries.[71] Intercommoning by nomadic people is still a feature of life in Mongolia but was largely eliminated in England perhaps as early as the medieval period.

Sneath has also suggested that religious values that predate Buddhism influenced attitudes to land in Mongolia during much of its history. Herders believed that the owners of the land were spirits known as *gajryneled* and not humans. These spirits were treated as high dignitaries and given offerings in ceremonies known as *oboo*. Typically, the *tsagaanluu* or white dragon had to be offered white food, such as dairy products and rice.[72] Such ceremonies were followed by sporting festivals that included wrestling contests. Today communal use remains a controversial topic, with the land issue differentiating new liberal parties that seek land privatization and more traditional and left parties that oppose this. In neighboring Chinese-controlled Inner Mongolia, mining is displacing herders and indigenous people from their communal land. Similar conflicts between communal agricultural use of land or hunting and the needs of high-growth economies to extract metals, minerals, and fossil fuels can be found in many parts of the world.

Communal land control is also a major political topic in India and is part of a long but far from unchanging tradition. In India, certainly in both the Punjab and the south, communal management was widespread and had varied forms. As in Mongolia, central authorities, including the Mogul empire, attempted to regulate communal land holdings, but informal and largely unmanaged commons between villages remained significant. Minoti Chakravarty-Kaul notes that the British authorities tried to formalize land ownership during the nineteenth century because they believed that this was necessary to raise agricultural productivity. The construction of large-scale irrigation projects allowed new land to be cultivated, and the introduction of railways led to rapid change in the Punjab. In particular, what the British termed waste, which was land on long fallow used by nomadic pastoralists, was taken under the legal control of local villages. The British placed great emphasis on tracing the family lineage of villagers. Although common land remained important, the British limited the use of the commons to those individuals who could prove that their ancestors had lived in the village to which the common land was attached. Nomadic peoples, who did not reside in one area, were prevented from using the commons that they had traditionally shared on a seasonal basis.[73]

The British authorities were keen to introduce private property rights and strengthen traditions that were closer to private ownership than collective provision across the whole country. E. P. Thompson quotes his own father, who notes, "The same era that saw the English peasant expropriated from his common lands saw the Bengal peasant made a parasite in his own country."[74] The younger Thompson further argues that "One need not be a specialist in the complexities of South Asian agrarian systems to see that these disputants were trying to compress their features into a modernising—or 'improving' English mask."[75] He believed that English enclosure of the commons to increase agricultural productivity was thus extended to English colonies like India.

The ecologist Madhav Gadgil and historian Ramachandra Guha note the devastating effects both socially and environmentally of the 1878 Indian Forest Act. This wiped out centuries of customary rights to forest commons. Much forestry was transformed into state property, which could be used for industrial timber production. Villages saw their access severely reduced, and industrial forestry meant that biodiverse woodland was transformed into monoculture to produce train sleepers and other lucrative timber products for the British empire.[76] During World War II, the Indian forests were extensively mined: in 1944 alone, the defense department took 909,000 tonnes of timber.[77]

Although commons still existed at Indian independence in 1947, they were both eroded and had moved, as in the English and Mongolian examples, from predominantly informal local management to greater central control. More recently in India, forests commons have been recognized in new legislation, but corruption has often led to legal conditions being ignored as land is taken from local communities and enclosed. The novelist Arundhati Roy has described the conflict between Maoist forces in east India and the central government as being focused on attempts by mining companies to seize indigenous communally managed forestland.[78] Her work illustrates that control of communal land is a recurring source of often violent conflict. Despite enclosure, commons remain an important part of the economic life of millions of Indian citizens.

English, Indian, and Mongolian commons have been part of an intellectual contest for land rights, with supporters in all three countries arguing that commons are successful and opponents suggesting they are failed ways of maintaining resources. Next, we look in more detail at these claims that commons are likely to succeed or fail in environmental terms.

Successful Commons

There are a number of well-researched accounts of commons, which have proved to be ecologically sustainable over long periods. For example, Elinor Ostrom discusses the village of Törbel, Switzerland, as an example of successful common-pool property management over many centuries. Törbel is a village of about six hundred people high in the Swiss Alps. Privately owned plots for growing fruit and vegetables are part of a mosaic of land ownership with a large common-pool element, and cattle are pastured on communally owned land. In this book *Balancing on an Alp: Ecological Change and Continuity in a Swiss Mountain Community*, anthropologist Robert Netting notes that records of land ownership patterns can be traced back to the thirteenth century.[79] As Elinor Ostrom observes:

Written legal documents dating back to 1224 provide information regarding the types of land tenure and transfers that have occurred in the village and rules used by the villages to regulate the five types of communally owned property: the alpine grazing meadows, the forests, the "waste" lands, the irrigation systems, and the paths and roads connecting privately and communally owned properties.[80]

In February 1483, the citizens signed an agreement to form an association with formal rules to manage their common property more effectively. The existing commoners could decide whether outsiders were allowed to join their community. The commons were strictly regulated. Netting observes that "no citizen could send more cows to the alp than he could feed during the winter."[81] Rules that are still in existence in the twenty-first century imposed substantial fines on commoners who overgrazed pastures. The overgrazing rule was easy to monitor and enforce; it simply involved counting cattle and punishing those who broke the rule by grazing more than they were allowed. All the citizens who owned cattle met once a year to change the rules if necessary and to select officials. The officials monitored the common, imposed fines, arranged manure distribution, and organized the rebuilding if huts or fences were damaged by avalanches. The harvesting of trees in the communally owned forest area was also regulated to prevent abuse. Meadows, gardens, and grain fields were owned privately but distributed among citizens on an equal basis. For much of the period, population was regulated to prevent unsustainable increase, and this was accomplished by "late marriages, celibacy, long birth spacing and considerable emigration."[82]

Netting argues that these arrangements maintained the productivity of the land around Törbel for many centuries and that clear rules and community involvement led to a sustainable system of land management. Around 80 percent of the land in Törbel remains communally owned today.

Ostrom's second example of historical commons is drawn from the work of Margaret McKean's study of three Japanese villages—Hirano, Nagaike, and Yamanaka. Törbel and the three Japanese villages share a similar environment—steep mountains with communal land and individually owned gardens. "Waste" produced timber, thatch for roofing, animal fodder, fertilizer, charcoal, and firewood. Many of the features of Törbel were similar to the Japanese commons although in Japan land ownership was a little more complex. For example, local large elite landowners could regulate some access to communal land and resources. Landowners appointed agents to regulate land use in the commons, but peasants over time asserted their right to establish their own rules for management of the land.

As in other communal systems, in the three Japanese villages, collective labor was necessary to maintain some features of the commons, and each household was obliged to help with collective labor to maintain the commons. For example, once a year the land had to be burnt to remove weeds and undergrowth, and three-meter firebreaks were needed to stop the fire from getting out of control. The fires had to be carefully monitored, and sometimes firefighting was necessary. All these tasks involved donations of labor. Cutting of timber and thatch were other tasks that required volunteers. To maintain the system of free labor, accounts were kept to help make sure that each household contributed its share. Ill health, family crisis, and a lack of able-bodied adults were recognized as acceptable excuses for avoiding such chores; however, those who did not contribute were punished.[83]

Monitoring and punishing offenders were important. Although the means varied from village to village, commoners often hired "detectives" who patrolled the commons on horseback and arrested those in breach of the rules. Sanctions were graded. Minor infractions were be met by demands for sake that was used to supply communal parties. At the top of the scale, serious offenders who broke communal regulations suffered exclusion or exile. The success of regulation, argues Margaret McKean, depended on having rules that were agreed to by the commoners rather than imposed from outside.

A third historical case study of a long-term and environmentally sustainable commons comes from the Spanish irrigation system known as *huerta*. Communal gardens in dry areas were irrigated by communal systems of irrigation, some of which continued successfully for nearly a thousand years. Elinor Ostrom notes the existence of a commons agreement to regulate the use and maintenance of the Benacher and Faitanar canals. Eighty-four irrigators signed the agreement on May 29, 1435, at the monastery of St. Francis near Valencia. In the arid regions of Spain, agriculture would have been impossible without sophisticated systems of irrigation. Vincent Ostrom's initial work on commons came with his case study of communal management of water systems in California that were influenced by such Spanish water commons.

Elinor Ostrom examines several different examples of *huerta*, and all involve locally determined rules, effective monitoring, and a scale of increasing punishments for rule breaking. The farmers in the Valencia irrigation system met every two or three years to elect an official known as the *syndic*, whose responsibilities including enforcing the rationing of canal water.[84]

Finally, Elinor Ostrom notes the existence of the *zanjera* irrigation communities in the Philippines. They are at least two hundred years old and may have evolved from *huertas* during the Spanish occupation of the islands, either directly from Spain or via Mexico. A recent research report outlines how they still manage water collectively and sustainably.[85]

There are numerous examples of other sustainable commons. The German historian Stefan Brakensiek argues that Hauberge in the southern Westphalia demonstrated that common use could even guarantee a sustainable form of economy, which harmonized the needs of industry and agriculture.[86]

The area was dominated by the iron industry, and tanning was also important. Mountain land was made into common fields, and use was rotated over cycles of rotation. Oaks were planted and felled after fifteen years to produce charcoal and bark for tanning. The following summer, the land was burnt to fertilize the soil, and rye was planted. After harvesting, the remaining oak rootstocks budded, and pigs were put in the fields to clear the ground. Sheep and cattle followed in subsequent years, and the cycle began again.

Elinor Ostrom's case-study research suggested to her that eight conditions were necessary to make more successful and sustainable commons. First, clearly defined boundaries were important so that outsiders might be excluded. This meant that the community could control how individuals within in it could use the commons. Second, rules should be adapted to local needs. Third, the rules that were used to conserve the commons had to be agreed on by the commoners. Ostrom believed that if people were involved in constructing the rules, they were more likely to abide by them. Such participation also meant that the rules were more likely to be realistic than if they were created by individuals from outside of the community. Fourth, effective monitoring had to take place. Without monitoring, rule breaking could not be recorded and punished. Fifth, graduated sanctions were needed. Rule breaking would be met with a small punishment to warn rule breakers that they were doing wrong, but those who continued to break the rules (for example, by catching too many fish or grazing too many cows) would be punished more severely. Severe sanctions for first offenses might punish individuals for accidental overuse and would not be appropriate. Sixth, conflict resolution should be cheap and easy so that problems (such as disagreement over interpretation of rules) could be solved without too much cost. Seventh, the community had to be recognized by higher-level authorities because if others based in central government interfered, they might destroy the ability of the commoners to regulate their territory. Finally, "in the case of larger common-pool resources, organization in the form of multiple layers of nested enterprises, with small local CPRs at the base level," different commons at different levels would need to interact efficiently.[87]

Elinor Ostrom also uses comparative data from failed commons, generally of recent date, that tend to reinforce these tentative conclusions about how to prevent the "tragedy of the commons." Nonetheless, she was keen to stress that these were far from universal rules. Commons are likely to be diverse and to demand flexible forms of management to work sustainably.

Ecologically Failed Commons

It is surprisingly difficult to find ecologically failed commons. Elinor Ostrom has done some useful work in this area. Commons generally seem to work in a sustainable manner. What is more likely is that the commons are condemned on economic grounds for failing to raise productivity rather than maintain environmental quality. It more frequently happens that commons areenclosed and destroyed than that they fail because of internal management problems.

The metaphor of the tragedy is suggested more often than it is found in reality. Typically, it was assumed that many African commons were badly damaged by overuse, but what the environmental historian William Beinart describes as an "avalanche of studies" in range ecology has challenged this view. The Tribal Grazing Land Policy that was introduced in Botswana in the 1970s semiprivatized previous communal grazing rights and led to greater inequality and environmental degradation. According to Beinart, researchers also found the claim that Baringo in Kenya was degraded due to commons management of cattle was not backed up by botanical evidence. Kwazulu, South Africa, was noted as an example of degradation, but it saw environmental change with some species of grass declining while others became more common, but this provided evidence of change rather than damage. Beinart's summary of African environmental history suggests that Africans throughout history have transformed their wider environment and sometimes degraded it, but systems of local knowledge and regulation were generally successful in making commons environmentally sustainable.[88]

Margaret McKean studied historical and contemporary commons in Japan, which covered 12 million hectares in the Tokugawa period (1600–1867) and still covers around 3 million hectares today. She notes that she had "not turned up an example of a commons that suffered ecological destruction while it was still a commons."[89] Kirsten Ewers Andersen of the United Nations Food and Agriculture Organization has noted that research studies since the 1980s "clearly show that the commons differ from open access resources in that they have management and apply rules of local governance and that tragedies are *not* the usual outcome."[90]

E. P. Thompson challenges the arguments of enclosers, who sought to justify taking control and fencing in English woodland in the eighteenth century. He argues that the tragedy argument, despite "its commonsense air," overlooks "that the commoners themselves were not without commonsense." Thompson suggests, as does Elinor Ostrom, that commoners developed "a rich variety of institutions and community sanctions which have effected restraints and stints upon use."[91] He notes that "signs of ecological crisis in some English forests in the eighteenth century" were due to political and legal reasons rather than generic failure to manage commons. He and other researchers into the English commons have also claimed that the erosion of traditional forest institutions led to uncertainties—about how to manage woodland and who had the authority to regulate commons—that contributed to overuse.

The Boston Common has been cited as a typical example of Garrett Hardin's "tragedy of the commons," where according to the historian James Loewen, "the common pasture was hopelessly overgrazed" in the seventeenth century.[92] Yet this seems, at best, misleading. Although its use has changed radically over time, in the twenty-first century, it is a public park rather than agricultural land. The Boston Common has also been suggested as an example of the triumph of the well-managed commons. Originally indigenous land, the Boston Common was owned by an Englishman, the Reverend William Blackstone, who sold it to the Bostonians. By 1646, it was becoming seriously overgrazed, but local people met and arranged a stinting system to ration use. It was agreed that each individual could graze only one cow or four sheep. The rule was monitored and enforced by a town keeper, who received a fee for every animal grazed on the common. Decisions about the commons were made at town meetings that were open to all citizens. This proved a sustainable system for over a hundred fifty years. As one historian noted, "In the end there was nothing of the 'tragedy of the commons' on Boston Common."[93]

Tragedies have occurred on some occasions. It has been argued that overgrazing led to degradation of land in Arizona, and shooting wars broke out in some areas of the United States between cattle and sheep farmers. However, these were open commons and lacked management. The degradation that occurred has been linked to economic cycles, with market activity leading to cycles of boom and bust, a factor often forgotten by researchers.[94]

The environmental scientist Ian Simpson and his colleagues investigated an apparent example of commons failure in Iceland. According to some estimates, Iceland has lost 40 percent of its topsoil, and forest cover has fallen to almost nothing. The summer mountain grazing commons at the bottom of glaciers, known as *afréttur*, have been blamed in part. The Icelandic landscape, which was once dominated by woodland, has been described as ovigenic (*oves* is Latin for "sheep") because it was thought that overgrazing by sheep led to the degradation of silty soils and loss of tree cover. Simpson and his colleagues found that the commons were well regulated. The Gregas or Grey Goose laws that can be traced back to the Icelandic Commonwealth between 930 and 1262 established a strong institutional structure to avoid overgrazing. Any commoner using an *afréttur* could call for an independent assessment of grazing capacity. Assessors then established the maximum sustainable number of animals that could be grazed. Farmers who shared the common land were given individual quotas and could be fined heavily if they went over their quota. The ownership of sheep was established via ear marks. Periods of fallow, when grazing was prohibited, were required, and new farmers could join the commons only with the agreement of existing members. The documentary sources thus indicate that Iceland followed "tightly defined regulation which includes defined boundaries and memberships, congruent rules, conflict resolution mechanisms and graduated sanctions . . . characteristic of successful management of common resources in other areas of the world."[95]

Nonetheless, the study of soil profiles and the use of a variety of environmental techniques illustrate that the commons system did not always prevent soil erosion. Simpson and his colleagues are unsure why the regulated Iceland commons led to environmental failure, but they have suggested that cultural knowledge may have stagnated. Sustainable management worked initially, but in later periods, environmental or social changes meant that regulation needed to be updated. Changing circumstances may have required new rules for communing, but this may not have occurred, leading to soil erosion and vegetation loss. Although the study does not provide an answer to why the commons at least partially failed, it illustrates that the relationship between land management and environmental quality is complex.

There are other examples of managed commons failure, as opposed to open-access commons failure. English agricultural reformers in the nineteenth century, such as Arthur Young, identified degradation, which they felt justified enclosure. For example, at Wildmore Fen in Lincolnshire, stints, which were supposed to ration use, had not been maintained, and too many animals were using the land. Horses were left to survive during hard winters without adequate shelter. Drainage was poorly organized, so the land regularly flooded. The picture was a bleak one:

they are extremely wet and unprofitable in their present state, standing much in need of drainage, are generally overstocked, and dug up for turf and fuel. The cattle and sheep depastured upon them are often very unhealthy, and of an inferior sort, occasioned by the scantiness, as well as the bad quality of their food, and the wetness of their lair. Geese, with which these commons are generally stocked . . . are often subject to be destroyed. It is not a constant practice with the commoners to take all their cattle off the fens upon the approach of winter; but some of the worst of the neat cattle, with the horses,—and particularly those upon Wildmore Fen,—are left to abide the event of the winter season; and it seldom happens that of the neat cattle many escape the effects of a severe winter. The horses are driven to such distress for food that they eat up every remaining dead thistle, and are said to devour the hair off the manes and tails of each other and also the dung of geese.[96]

Such accounts suggest that if commons rule are not well designed and stuck to productivity will fall. Ostrom's work also illustrates that commons could break down.

The historian Jeanette Neeson argues that those who wish to see the commons enclosed identify problems and that those who defend commons identify benefits. Anecdotal evidence is thus used in a biased partisan fashion. She suggests that pressure from advocates of enclosure could lead to degradation. As commons are enclosed, more stress is put on existing commons, and they tend to be less well managed. Poorer management and damage are then used to justify more enclosure.[97] In India, as Minoti Chakravarty-Kaul notes, the enclosure process could create a real "tragedy of the commons" because commons became marginalized and overused.[98]

John Locke, the seventeenth-century English political philosopher, discusses indigenous land use as an example of the failure of commons and the need for private property. He cites material growth rather than environmental quality as the appropriate criteria. He notes that "the wild Indian, . . . knows no enclosure, and is still a tenant in common" before observing that lack of private property and productive labor meant that "a king of a large and fruitful territory there, feeds, lodges, and is clad worse than a day-laborer in England."[99]

The question of why commons fail and what is meant by failure is less easy to answer than might be thought. Success and failure depend on the criteria used. The nineteenth-century criticism of English commons was based not on environmental quality but on productivity and even social judgment. This consideration means we must consider notions of culture and power in assessing commons. There is no value-free yardstick that can define the success or failure of commons. Many apparently neutral attempts to measure the success or failure of commons are biased by particular assumptions, which at the very least need to be made visible and examined if they are to be convincingly assessed. Discussion of the commons demands discussion of culture, which is the subject of the next chapter.

2

Culture in Common?

To the medieval mind such landscapes were liminal places, where humanity might encounter the supernatural . . . in early medieval Scandinavian cosmology, where the utgard (the same term was used of the common waste beyond the farmland) was inhabited by monsters and was dark. . . . The association of wilder spaces beyond cultivation with spiritual or mythical sites is a global phenomenon, reflected in the widespread occurrence of sacred groves and forests, or revered mountains and rivers, often subject, . . . to communal forms of guardianship. . . . They were spaces where ritual, such as the "beating of the bounds," with its attendant claiming of boundary markers, took place and folk memory played a vital part. Minor features in the landscape, both natural and man-made, along the open boundaries across common land were claimed and named. Symbolism was often powerful: the liminality of the common waste was reflected in its association with the dead, notably as the places of gallows and gibbets.[1]

The discovery that one's home or business is on the site of an old Indian graveyard is a horror movie cliché. Many ghost stories (such as those of M. R. James) involve the arrival of ancient spirits that have been antagonized by the taking of property. Disrupting long-held communal rights to land might be seen to stir up supernatural forces, and such apparent superstitions and rumors may have a functional basis. The rational management of the commons is helped, perhaps, by appeals to the irrational. Christopher Rodgers and his colleagues researched the environmental history of English and Welsh commons and note that commons were associated with the supernatural and the irrational. The boundary of a commons was often a boundary between the wild of the waste and the tamed cultivated fields.

This question of how culture, including social norms and human institutions, helps or hinders an understanding of the historical commons and future sustainable history is the subject of this chapter. Culture is a vast, complex, and shifting area of discussion that is perhaps easier to ignore, and any attempt to deal with it is likely to be incomplete at best. Even defining the term *culture* is difficult. The literary theorist Terry Eagleton notes that it "is said to be one of the two or three most complex words in the English language."[2] In this context, culture deals with the beliefs and practices relating to the management and meaning of the commons. The writer and activist David Korten has developed a useful description:

Culture is the system of beliefs, values, perceptions, and social relations that encodes the shared learning of a particular human group essential to individual survival and orderly social function. It serves as the interpretive lens through which the human brain processes the massive flow of data from our senses to distinguish the significant from the inconsequential, assign meaning, and shape our behavior: "This plant will kill you. That one is food." . . . The processes by which culture shapes our perceptions and behavior occur mostly at an unconscious level. It rarely occurs to us to ask whether the reality we perceive through the lens of the culture within which we grew up is the "true" reality. We just take for granted that it is.[3]

An illustration of the cultural underpinnings of commons comes from the Maine lobster fishing grounds in New England. Fishing is a classic example of the "tragedy of the commons," and efforts to regulate fishing at an international level (such as European Union's Commons Fisheries Policy) often fail. The anthropologist James Acheson suggests that the Maine lobster fishery, which is regulated by local people, provides a model of management that might be applied more widely to enhance sustainability. For generations, local lobster catchers have maintained a commons, rationing access to prevent the lobsters from being overexploited. Acheson argues that while the management makes economic and environmental sense, cultural factors are important in making it work. Strong traditions and norms are used to make this sustainable system function. For example, there is strong hostility to new fishers. According to Acheson, it takes a long time to be accepted as a fisher, and even those who belong to local fishing families may have difficulty joining the community. He suggests that it is best to start young to learn the norms of the lobster community as one grows up. Those who break the most important taboo of interfering with another lobsterer's fishing gear were unlikely to last long in the industry. Such norms, Acheson argues, are essential to prevent overexploitation.[4] Many other writers, including Elinor Ostrom and E. P. Thompson, have emphasized the role of informal norms or customs, as opposed to formal codified law, in the creation and continuation of historic and modern commons.

William Cronon's account of the mutual incomprehension between indigenous and colonial peoples in New England in the seventeenth century is another good illustration of the significance of culture.[5] The arriving Europeans saw the indigenous people as impoverished and were amazed at how few material goods they used in the midst of a fertile and apparently highly productive landscape. In the eyes of the newcomers, the indigenous people's failure to enrich themselves justified European control of the landscape. In summary, the colonialists argued that because the indigenous failed to maximize their prosperity by using the land, Europeans were right to take the land and use it more productively to generate greater wealth. As has already been noted, the philosopher John Locke used this argument to justify taking their land. The indigenous felt that the Europeans were foolish to work as hard as they did and noted their failure, at least at first, to prepare for harsh winters by storing supplies, which they believed would lead to disaster. The lack of physical material possessions made it easier for the indigenous to move with seasonal changes and sustain themselves through cold winters. People from the two cultures held different assumptions regarding what was sustainable or good and what was proper land use and economic benefit.

Words like *benefit*, *cost*, and *prosperity* are to some extent cultural and cannot be determined with precision as scientific or neutral terms. This insight is important if we are to understand the value of commons. Karl Marx, as has been noted, argued that the earth should be passed on in "an improved state to succeeding generations."[6] This is an important but problematic suggestion because without a discussion about the broad category of culture, it is difficult to determine what is meant by "improved state." Marx's otherwise rather concise definition of the apparently sustainable and prosperous ecological commons could suggest both "green" readings of Marx and hyperindustrializing approaches based on "raising the productive forces" and remaking nature. An ecological Marx might have very different implications for sustainability than a Marx that placed greater emphasis on raising the forces of production and introducing rapid industrialization. Although there has been a spirited debate on the ecological contributions of Marx and Engels, this is not the key issue here.[7] Whatever Marx's intention, the word *improved* is open to interpretation. After all, building a factory and growing a flower meadow are both forms of economic improvement. *Improvement* is a value-laden term that differs in exact meaning from one society to another and among different groups within any individual society.

The nineteenth-century English agricultural reformer Arthur Young challenged the commons because he felt that "commons" made "improvement" less likely. This is subtly or not so subtly different from assessing whether a commons is ecologically sustainable. The ecological commons might or might not be possible, but even if sustainable, it may not be compatible with improvement. Improvement, in turn, is not a simple measurable assumption but is strongly shaped by social norms. The interaction between culture and economics has to be discussed if the concept of commons is to be understood and a sustainable history of the future advanced. The cultural assumptions behind economic analysis of the commons must be understood because economics is also cultural rather than an unproblematically neutral social science.

Commons as an Economic Solution

Elinor Ostrom notes that although Garrett Hardin was a biologist, he shared the assumption of most economists that human beings focus on personal gain and find cooperation difficult. She also observes that Hardin echoes the logic of the distinguished economist H. Scott Gordon, who argues that "fish in the sea are valueless to the fisherman, because there is no assurance that they will be there for him tomorrow if they are left behind today."[8]

Economists claim that their subject is a value-free social science, but their critics argue that it is based on particular beliefs that may be open to discussion and interpretation. These are worth briefly outlining to help explain the strengths and potential weaknesses of this approach to examining commons. The word *economics* is derived from the study of *oikos*, the ancient Greek word for "household." According to Lionel Robbins's well-known definition, economics "is the science which studies human behavior as a relationship between given ends and scarce means which have alternative uses."[9] Economists focus on concepts such as choice, resources, rationality, and opportunity cost, all of which are seen as neutral rather than culturally determined and can be applied universally to different human societies. It is assumed that human beings need to make choices. In fact, the concept of choice is perhaps the essence of economics. Resources that can be used to produce goods or services can be used in different ways, and we must choose how to use such resources. Opportunity cost is the notion that when one choice is made, other choices are given up. The choice or choices that are not made are the opportunity cost. There also is a strong assumption of rationality, within economics, which stresses that individuals pick the alternatives that provide them with the most personal gain. The sociologist Erik Olin Wright notes that "economists assign a privileged place to self-interested rational action in their micro-level explanations of social phenomenon, and thus give central weight to the problem of incentives in explaining variations across contexts."[10]

Implicit in economics is the notion of methodological individualism, which the political philosopher Jon Elster has defined in the following terms: "The elementary unit of social life is the individual human action. To explain social institutions and social change is to show how they arise as the result of the actions and interaction of individuals."[11] The interaction of communities is largely ignored by economists, who may find it difficult to understand collective forms of property and communal action.

Economists argue that individual choice determines outcomes. If more consumers are prepared to pay for a product, for example, then such increased demand tends to push up the price. Price increases tend to increase profits and motivate producers to provide what consumers desire. Individual preferences based on the need to gain the maximum personal benefit drive the economic system. Individuals compete to try to achieve the greatest personal benefit. The commons, in its varied forms, seems to cut across many of these assumptions because of the apparent free-rider problem. Garrett Hardin and others critical of common-pool property arrangements argue that in a commons, individuals will take advantage of those who might conserve a resource by using it more intensively. Apparently selfish behavior from a free rider is perversely rewarded, and economists assume that an individual cannot trust other individuals to conserve shared ground. Thus, those who act ethically and attempt to promote sustainability (say, by removing their cattle from the commons) will see the commons destroyed if others continue to put their cattle on it. The rational individual may even put more cattle on the commons, exploiting the good action of the supposedly moral individual. Self-interest pushes ethical action to the margins and, as Garrett Hardin argues, means that commons must be eliminated if land is to be sustained ecologically. Erik Olin Wright suggests that for economists, "a well-maintained commons is a puzzle" and as such "cries out for an explanation." He notes that economists tend to be surprised and confused that commons might work.[12]

In contrast, Elinor Ostrom has used assumptions of broadly rational methical individualism to suggest that in particular circumstances commons can be maintained to sustain shared prosperity. Individuals can join together and agree to maintain conservation processes, especially where sanctions can be applied and rules are mutually agreed on rather than imposed by outsiders. In some circumstances, the commons can provide an economically rational solution to resource management.

Elinor Ostrom might be seen as moving beyond economics in her largely economic account of commons. There are number of reasons to see her approach as more sophisticated and flexible than previous attempts by economists to analyze common-pool property. However, she has been criticized as an "economic imperialist" who applies the notions of traditional economics to areas of human life where they are inappropriate. Rather than making economics more cultural, she might be seen as making social and cultural matters part of the economic approach of costs, benefits, and rational maximizing behavior.[13] Elinor Ostrom's theoretical approach to economics, developed with her husband, Vincent, needs to be understood if we are to assess her description of commons in terms of its relationship to questions of culture.

The Ostroms are various described as members of the Bloomington school or new economic institutionalism (NEI) or as advocates of institutional analysis and development (IAD). Bloomington refers to the main Indiana University campus where the Ostroms were both based. IAD is the particular variant of new economic institutionalism developed by the Ostroms. NEI is a product of market-based economics that is rooted in the thought of individuals like Austrian economists such as Friedrich Hayek and Ludwig von Mises, whose assumptions seem much closer to those of Garrett Hardin than Ostrom.[14] As has been noted, Ludwig von Mises specifically criticized the concept of common-pool property. Elinor Ostrom was even a president of the Public Choice Society. Public choice is an approach to governance that is strongly critical of the state and advocates market-based policies such as privatization. Rational-choice theory is at the heart of public-choice theory and NEI, an approach that seeks to extend economic reasoning, based on costs and benefits, to sociology to explain human behavior outside areas normally covered by economics. Elinor and her husband, Vincent, took rational-choice theory in a new direction. They were also influenced by more unorthodox voices, including the economist John R. Commons, who focused on the "bundle of property rights" concept.[15] NEI is based on the assumption that rationality is "bounded"—that is, individuals follow self-interest but within a particular context that is shaped by particular values and circumstances.

The new institutionalist economists bring in the influence of particular institutions and varied culture. They build on concepts such as rational choice but apply them in what they see as a messy, complex, and often rather irrational world. From the perspective of much traditional economics, this is boldly radical; from that of disciplines such as sociology and anthropology, it remains rather conservative. Maximizing behavior (rather than alternative goals) continues to drive the models.

Elinor Ostrom argues that property rights are not simply state or private and that, in many circumstances, it is impractical to replace commons with private property. Through negotiation and learning, individuals can often get together and find ways of managing common property so that, through collective action, individuals can maximize their net collective benefit. From her perspective, failure to work out common rules and apply them would lead to the destruction of the commons, so self-interest is served by establishing consensual frameworks. Such consensual construction of effective rules may be difficult to achieve in some circumstances but is not impossible. Elinor Ostrom rejected the approach of unrefined rational-choice theory that suggests that cooperation is virtually impossible because of the prisoners' dilemma and similar models that invoke the free-rider problem.

The Icelandic economist Thráinn Eggertsson sums up the new institutional approach to commons by noting that commons are often economically efficient but their relative benefits depend on social and political factors as well as pure economic considerations.[16] This approach is a form of political economy in that political assumptions and institutions are seen as shaping economic decision making. The rules depend on the institutions constructed, and institutional design is a political act. Even at the level of a Japanese village or indigenous territory in the Ecuadorian Amazon, the politics of rulemaking and negotiation is apparent. The political institutions used to maintain a commons are based on the development of particular cultures, which are refined, are transmitted from generation to generation, and evolve over time. Such cultural foundations of an economic system are generally ignored by economists but were of vital importance to Elinor Ostrom.

Culture as a Means of Conservation

Elinor Ostrom's research has uncovered numerous examples of the cultural reinforcement of conservation mechanisms used to maintain commons in a sustainable fashion. Drawing on theories of evolutionary cooperation, she argues that cooperative forms of behavior have tended to be selected for throughout human history. Although societies throughout history and prehistory have been diverse, they all have had to solve collective problems such as how to provide food, protect their communities, and look after the young. Ostrom argues that during the Pleistocene, from three million years ago to approximately ten thousand years before the present, human beings lived as hunter-gatherers in small bands. To survive, societies needed to learn who to trust and who to treat with caution. Whether societies were based on "stronger dominance hierarchies or by looser social exchange networks," those "who solved these problems most effectively would have had a selective advantage over those who did not."[17] However, she has reservations about simply applying an evolutionary approach, without further evidence, and draws on experimental data that also suggested, she believed, that norms reinforcing cooperative behavior are likely to be promoted.[18]

There are numerous historical examples of norms within commons that tend to encourage shared cooperative behavior. Canadian First Nations scholar Christopher Hannibal-Paci's examination of the conservation of sturgeon by the Cree and Ojibwe is a good illustration of how such norms reinforce sustainable economic activity. He notes how both archeological evidence and historical data, including oral history, show that sturgeon were a mainstay of the local indigenous economies for at least four thousand years around Lake Winnipeg, Manitoba, Canada. The lake fisheries were a commons used by indigenous people until commons rights were removed during the colonial era. In recent years, overfishing has been a problem. As private property rights and commodification of fisheries have been increased, sturgeon catches have fallen. The most fruitful attempts to restore sustainable use of sturgeon have, according to Hannibal-Paci, been achieved through recreating commons.

He notes how cultural practices (including a strong norm of sharing) were used to encourage sustainable management of fish stocks by the indigenous. Although he does not refer to Ostrom's work, his conclusions provide a historical example of her observation that rational economic management may be aided by cultural norms as well as formal rules. Indigenous knowledge about sturgeon was passed from parents to children, with fishing techniques moving from one generation to the next. The Cree and Ojibwe were well informed about fishing methods, spawning sites, and sturgeon behavior. Families gathered to catch and process the sturgeon every spring, using every part of the fish in one way or another.

Christopher Hannibal-Paci suggests that communal management of the lake fisheries was encouraged by a culture that strongly reinforced sharing:

Fishers would *bring home* the fish, tethered live or processed (butchered or smoked), and give to family relations. The purpose of a sharing network has been misunderstood by historians and anthropologists who equated sharing as a reasonable response to a *brutish short existence*. What these scholars fail to consider is that ethical systems based on learning develop, fishers learn that co-operation far outweighs any sort of benefit resulting from competition. Similar to understandings derived from the *Prisoners Dilemma* framework, sharing results in the greatest pay-offs in reciprocal relations. Sharing sturgeon extended from immediate family members, close relatives, community members and eventually to the settler newcomers. Co-operation-sharing also formed, for a time, the basis for trade relations in the later 1700's. Within reserve communities, up to present, sharing still served the function of cementing the esteem and value of a fisher/hunter to feed others.[19]

There are many similar examples. The economist Jean-Philippe Platteau cites the Mossi, an ethnic group in Burkina Faso, and the lagoon fishers of Bahia in Brazil. In both situations, commons have been maintained with reference to strong social codes that encourage careful shared use of collective property based on "an ethical code of honor and social respect." Platteau cites Badini, who notes that the Mossis followed a social code called the *moaga*: "Since a person can only exist through collective opinion, it is collective opinion that rates people and rare are those who are willing to incur the risk to defy it. The point is that its verdict is merciless and without appeals."[20]

Margaret McKean notes that Japanese commons were policed by detectives who were hired by the commoners. Individual commoners who broke rules were fined in money or saki.[21] German commons in the nineteenth century were often governed cooperatively by peasants. Officials such as the herdsman and the reeve made sure that grazing was sustainable. Strong cultural practices cemented these German commons. Community life was lively, and a calendar of events included the beating of the bounds, which was

an annual procession around the boundaries of the village and the lands belonging to it, a communal drink after auditing the common box (the community funds). Folk customs were combined with the common pasture. To the peasants, the bell that the village bull wore around his neck on the pasture signaled, "the reeve is coming, the reeve is coming!" (The reeve kept the community's breeding bull.) On New Year's Day, the herdsmen blew their horns, went from door to door and sang their songs, asking peasants to give them something—such as their best-smoked sausages. The gifts were considered an expression of the peasants' esteem for the community employees' careful handling of their livestock.[22]

Examples can be multiplied of riddles, folk practices, and religious rituals that provide norms that encourage careful use of the commons. The widespread existence of sacred groves of trees, which were contained within commons rather than privately owned, protected them from exploitation in many parts of the world, including Africa and India. The Mongolian commons, as is noted in the previous chapter, were protected by the notion that supernatural beings were the real owners of land and had to be respected. Indeed, appeals to religion are often used to promote conservation within commons. The Indian institutional economist Anil Gupta noted that in Niger, fishing sanctuaries known as *guntu* are regulated partly by religious practices. Annual rituals known as Do and Sorko are used to keep the river gods happy, and those who break the fishing rules by fishing in the sanctuary waters are punished. Minor offenses are met by shaming, more serious offenses by fines, and repeat offenders can be excluded from the communal fishing grounds. The *guntu* is an area of deep river that is particularly important for fish stocks to regenerate within. The river gods must be worshipped to make sure that they cooperate to maintain fish levels in the *guntu*. In recent decades, the noise from motor boats upset the gods, so prayers were needed to ask for forgiveness.

Anil Gupta further argues that although complex, such culture capital is functional for sustained prosperity, noting that "myths act as memory cells of the organization of the social groups."[23] Myth can be seen as rational if it is used to sustain the environment. In turn, economic rationality is served by ecological sustainability, and religion can be part of the cement that keeps communities together or via taboos that prevent the overexploitation of trees, fish and other environmental resources. Spelling out the meaning of myth, however, may destroy the power of the myth. When the sacred becomes scientific, it loses its potency, and the removal of mystery leads to degradation of the environment.

Informal social conventions may also help preserve the commons. For example, Elinor Ostrom notes that "Shaming and honoring are very important. We do not have as much of an understanding of that. There are scholars who understand that, but that's not been part of our accepted way of thinking about collective action."[24] The nineteenth-century jurist Sir Henry Maine, who studied the origins of law and was fascinated by indigenous societies, felt that customary law was so strongly held that it became instinctive and as such was "almost as blind and unconscious as that which produces some of the movements of our bodies."[25] From this perspective, such norms, internalized as customary law, may be almost invisible. They become part of the fabric of life and are often far more powerful than formal rules recognized by lawyers and politicians.

Culture versus Economics

The argument that commons can be assessed using a theoretical framework based on economic rationality initially seems convincing. Elinor Ostrom and other new institutional economists use historical data to draw lessons for a sustainable future. They establish that far from being irrational or primitive, commoners throughout history developed sophisticated ways of managing environmental resources that were often efficient and sustainable. Cultural norms reinforced such sustainability, and norms as much as formal rules discouraged individuals from free-riding. A close examination of this approach, however, suggests that the reality of commons may be less simple. It is laudable that commoners are not dismissed as irrational, yet many social scientists feel that the assumption of rationality, even in a bounded form, used by the new institutionalists remains crude.

Ostrom's approach can also appear rather simplistically functionalist. If something exists, it is assumed that it has evolved over a period of historical time: thus, what exists is good because social evolution has made it so. One danger with this line of thought, attractive as it might first appear, is that it assumes a process of historical evolution that selects against the dysfunctional. This is problematic because commons may take diverse forms and in many situations commons have disappeared. As is discussed in the next chapter, commons often disappear not because of functional failure but because they are enclosed and destroyed against the wishes of commoners. Even in the absence of enclosure and removal, commons change over time and not simply as a result of the needs of commoners who develop better forms of management. Too great an emphasis on economics and an assumption of functional evolution can, at the very least, oversimplify an understanding of the history of commons.

It also seems to be too narrow an account for describing the various ways that culture might be functional in maintaining norms that, in turn, deliver rational environmental management. A variety of religions and sets of beliefs have different influences on the environment. The religious ceremonies undertaken by commoners may not always work to protect the commons. There is a larger debate about the relationship between sustainability and theology, with critics suggesting that some religious traditions may help accelerate environmental degradation rather than work to support sustainable use. Typically, the Abrahamic religions, which include Judaism, Christianity, and Islam, have been seen as ecologically dysfunctional and as having values that reject sustainable management. They have been criticized as displacing earlier pagan religions that promoted sustainable practices.

It has been argued that they see the material world of nature as tainted by sin, believe that the rest of nature should be exploited by humanity, and stress a God-given domination of humanity over other species. The historian Lynn White, Jr., who argues this position fervently in his essay entitled *The Historic Roots of the Ecologic Crisis*, notes the Biblical injunction shared by Jews, Christians, and Muslims from Genesis 1.28: "God blessed them, and said to them, 'Be fruitful and multiply; fill the earth and subdue it; have dominion over the fish of the sea, over the birds of the air, and over every living thing that moves on the earth.'"

White argues that we shall "have a worsening ecologic crisis until we reject the Christian axiom that nature has no reason for existence save to serve man."[26] But White's argument has been criticized by those who suggest that the religions of the book may contain ecological wisdom. There are traditions of stewardship in the Bible and environmentally friendly interpretations of Judaism based on the Old Testament.[27] There are also strikingly "green" passages in the Koran (such as the injunction to reject wasteful use of resources in Surah 5, verse 141) that give rise to ecological interpretations of Islam.[28] Islam has been used to promote sustainable common fisheries management in Zanzibar.[29] The Catholic theologian John Hart has discussed at some length the Biblical roots of a sacramental commons.[30] Drawing on Hart's thesis, it has been argued that people who worship and respect God should work for the common good, which involves promoting human equality, pursuing justice, and respecting the environment. Thus, we must protect the environment because God demands that we act as "stewards of the earth."[31]

The debate between those who see religions as having an environmentally beneficial dimensional and those who reject this assumption will no doubt continue, but it seems a little eccentric to explain social practices (including religion) predominantly in terms of their perceived economic or environmental rationality. Religion is just one subset of the vast field of culture, and religious practices seem far too diverse to interpret in terms of their likely rationality-inducing power within the field of commons management.

A related problem with Elinor Ostrom's framework is that this more sophisticated approach to economics tends to point to a break with economics. If people seek to maximize benefits or minimize costs(which remains an *if*), such benefits and costs can be defined only within a given context. As has been shown, she suggests that shared norms (that is, culture) reinforce the good management of the commons, but it seems that cultural factors shape what is seen as useful. The utility of a good or service or the indifference between choices varies depending on goals that themselves are culturally determined. It may be that it is impossible to separate culture from economics. Culture is very diverse, and it is problematic that economists generally assume a homogeneous world where self-interest rules condition all decision making. This is misleading because commons have existed within the context of societies with alternative logics. Indeed, anthropologists have identified the widespread existence of gift economies based on systems of social sharing rather individual maximizing behavior. Such gift economies need to be considered if we are to deepen our understanding of common-pool property systems.

The Gift Economy

Adam Smith famously observed that "It is not from the benevolence of the butcher, the brewer, or the baker, that we expect our dinner but from their regard to their own interests."[32] Self-interest and rational calculation can thus look like common sense, but there are other ways of understanding human motivations. In 1981, ten Irish republican prisoners starved themselves to death to win the right to be seen as political prisoners rather than criminals. Sacrifice of life might be seen as the ultimate rejection of economic rationality, but this has not prevented economists from trying to explain the behavior of, for example, suicide bombers using this assumption. The economists Karen Pittel and Dirk Rübbelke argue that "that although a terrorist gives up future utility from consumption by committing a suicide attack, this loss can be overcompensated by the utility he derives from the attack."[33]

The 1981 hunger strike by nationalists was part of a long Irish tradition of republicans starving themselves, sometimes to the point of death, as a political tactic.[34] Hunger strikes in Ireland reach back to the nineteenth century when a peasant might refuse food or even water at the gates of a local landowner; this was seen as a way of shaming the landowner in the face of his perceived failure to maintain the welfare of tenants. The roots of the hunger strike go back to ancient Brehon law. This was practiced in early medieval Ireland and governed, among other matters, the control of common land. Within Brehon law and Irish society, hospitality and sharing were part of a strong social code. Those who did not fulfill their social obligations were seen as pariahs, and the hunger strike was one, albeit extreme, means of shaming them. In his book *The Gift*, the sociologist Marcel Mauss shows that gift giving was a common form of economic activity.[35] Complex systems of obligation governed sharing and gift giving in numerous societies. One example is the potlatch, well known from the Northwest Pacific Coast region of North America among indigenous people. The social standing of individuals was established by their ability to throw huge parties as part of the potlatch. The gift economy is one in which social obligation and status are goals and economic activity is a means rather than an end. In the gift economy, the butcher and the baker might be embarrassed not to give because they would be seen as small individuals and unworthy. Gifts, according to Mauss, are never free; they create social obligations that must be fulfilled. Mauss suggests that social obligation rather than material improvement is the key motive in societies governed by such an economy.

This social dimension seems to be missing from Elinor Ostrom's account of the commons. Economic anthropology teaches us not to accept economic self-interest as a given. In fact, there is a major debate within economic anthropology as to the status of culture versus economics. Economic anthropology is a major field that deals with the potential historical record of commons. Its three major schools are formalism, substantivism, and culturalism, and all three focus on the relationship between culture and economics.[36] Elinor Ostrom's work takes place within a formalist framework. Formalism over laps with the new economic institutional approach, with formalists suggesting that economic activity follows broadly universal rules of maximizing behavior that are shaped by specific local institutions. Individuals seek to maximize their private benefit, societies may be diverse, but the basic assumptions of the modern economist apply universally. Humans seek to maximize net benefits, costly behavior is rejected, and the aim is to accumulate greater net gains. Although they share a concern with bounded rationality and a nuanced criticism of traditional economic assumptions, many formalists go beyond the basic assumptions of the new institutionalist school. Rationality is defined as rational in terms of accepted cultural norms within a society. Thus, rather than being driven by abstract economics, human action, while seeking to maximize benefit, will vary with diverse cultural norms.

The substantivist school, which originated with Karl Polanyi, a twentieth-century Hungarian intellectual, argues that economics in precapitalist societies is not separate from the rest of society but embedded within wider social behavior. Social goals, such as status achievement, drive economic decisions rather than the other way around. For example, gift giving might be a means of achieving high social status rather than economic accumulation. According to substantivists, the notion of a gift economy is vital to many societies; commons and social sharing are intrinsic in such accounts.

The cultural school within economic anthropology goes further than the substantivists and argues that economies are local and almost entirely cultural determined. Cultural assumptions are so varied that they cannot be studied in any meaningful way except locally. Universal rules are likely to be misleading. Anthropologists suggest that it is difficult to separate aspects of society such as economic, social, legal, and cultural. There is a danger of making artificial distinctions, which shines out from, for example, William Cronon's study of indigenous New England[37] and E. P. Thompson's account of commons history in England.[38] Economics is just one part of a whole way of life.

Contested Cultures

Cultures are contested, and values change over time for reasons that are probably ultimately mysterious to historians and social scientists. Different cultural beliefs may coexist within a society. Different social groups may seek to gain dominance through the propagation of different cultural assumptions. Values may be disputed: the term *culture wars* comes to mind. A sustainability culture war is occurring at present. The existence of anthropogenic climate change has been challenged by an alliance of conservative commentators. In some countries, such as the United States and Australia, it currently is difficult for politicians on the right of the political spectrum to endorse the scientific consensus. This skepticism (or as critics might say, denial) is linked to cultural values that endorse extractivism, which is the notion that resources like gas and oil should be taken from the earth and used with little or no concern for sustainability. This may be linked to "American" values and seen as part of a way of life that is dependent on high energy use. Although it might be argued that culture with its subjective element should not take priority over science and acceptance of the science of climate change may become more widespread on the right, the culture of extractivism would continue to shape responses to the problem of climate change even if accepted as such.

Culture, broadly and crudely defined, strongly shapes practices. At the very least, culture strongly influences the definition of economic. As has been noted, even in the formalist framework, which comes closest to traditional economics, costs and benefits are seen in terms of culturally specific goals. So within a commons, the goal might be to worship a god or goddess or provide a home for spirits rather than to achieve a more narrowly defined materialistic goal.

Even if a commons is maintained for a narrowly material motive, cultural assumptions might continue to shape the economic objective or objectives sought. In his book *Stone Age Economics*, the anthropologist Marshall Sahlins argues that even if *economics* is described in terms of meeting wants with given resources in a rational fashion, different assumptions of how to go about this might apply. According to Sahlins, hunter-gatherers, settled agricultural societies, and industrialized societies might all have very different logics. He argues that wants can be satisfied by either producing more or "desiring less." In a market-based developed economy, we aim to produce more goods and services, but Sahlins argues that there is a Zen Buddhist road to prosperity. Like the Buddhists, we could strive to desire less. The Zen approach suggests that human material wants are relatively limited and can be satisfied relatively easily:

Adopting the Zen strategy, a people can enjoy an unparalleled material plenty—with a low standard of living. That, I think, describes the hunters. And it helps explain some of their more curious economic behavior: their "prodigality" for example—the inclination to consume at once all stocks on hand, as if they had it made.[39]

Sahlins argues that by limiting wants and enjoying leisure, hunter-gatherers maintained their own culturally determined version of affluence: "The hunter, one is tempted to say, is an 'uneconomic man.' Consequently he is 'comparatively free of material pressures,' has no sense of possessions, shows an undeveloped sense of property, is completely indifferent to any material pressures, manifests a lack of interest in developing his technological equipment."[40]

In different contexts, the commons may limit the potential for economic accumulation and increase the potential for leisure and sustainable use of resources. Although the "tragedy of the commons" in many circumstances can be avoided, the measure of success of commons depends on culturally specific preferences between accumulation and leisure and between resource extraction and resource renewal.[41]

Jeanette Neeson's study of commons in England from 1700 to 1820 suggests that commons were often seen as damaging by those who felt that creating more potential for economic independence would help prevent socially defined abhorrent behavior. Neeson argues, as has been noted earlier, that it is necessary to use historical documents to assess the value of commons because defenders and detractors held different assumptions and used different criteria to assess the value of commons. Those who criticized the commons did so in terms of economic value in the market along with the efficient use of the resources. The commoners, in contrast, lived to some extent outside the market and valued their shared use of the land. It gave them economic security and allowed them to live more easily. They could graze their cattle and gather their firewood but were less worried by the market value expressed in currency. Neeson notes that much of what the commoners valued in the commons was invisible or ignored by critics of communing. The commoners "lived in part on the invisible earnings of grazing and gathering." However, the value of commons to the commoners was not something that their critics took into account, either "because they did not look or because they did not want to see." The English commoners were economically independent to some extent and used their independence to indulge in leisure pursuits that were abhorrent to many contemporary commentators. Commoners were often seen as "lazy, insubordinate and poor. Above all commons provided independence to some extent and with it greater freedom":

> From this freedom came time to spend doing things other than work. This is the evidence for the accusation by critics of commons that commoners were lazy. . . . Clearly sporting, indolence, laziness, taking time off, enjoying life, lack of ambition (all the words are loaded with values of one kind or another) had their origins in other things as well as a life outside the market economy.[42]

Christopher Rodgers and his colleagues observe that the seventeenth-century Puritans viewed commons as "great Nurseries of Idleness and Beggary" and cite the seventeenth-century mapmaker John Norden, who condemned the commons because it "attracted squatters living idle and godless lives."[43] Similar sentiments have been voiced about commoners (including indigenous) peoples the world over.

Although the agricultural reformer Arthur Young initially challenged commons as a barrier to agricultural improvement and advocated enclosure, he later defended commons as a means of reducing poverty. His change of heart came about as he became appalled at the effect that enclosure had on the welfare and independence of the commoners.[44] E. P. Thompson records that Young was told by a cottager in 1804 that "inclosing would ruin England; it was worse than ten wars. I kept four cows before the parish was inclosed, and now I do not keep so much as a goose."[45]

The example of Young's change of heart confirms that economic logic, however sophisticated, provides an inadequate analysis of common-pool property systems. Accumulation versus leisure and sustainable use versus extraction provide different standards for assessing the economic utility of commons. These different assumptions of what *economic value* means are ignored by purely economic accounts, however seemingly sophisticated, of the commons. Different social groups have different economic stakes in the commons. Even if it is nuanced and explicit about competing demands, economics does not exhaust the concept of commons. An alternative culture of commoning is illustrated by the anthropologist Veronica Strang's account of aboriginal commons in the far north of Queensland, Australia. The land, which is owned collectively by indigenous clans, is not an economic resource alone but is a magical landscape inhabited by ancestor spirits and other supernatural beings. Use is conditioned by a pagan assumption that the landscape is fundamentally alive and has agency. As a human being does, it has will and can make decisions. The land must be cared for by people who carry out a variety of actions, including in some places singing to the land. Modern technology and assumptions may flavor how such rituals are undertaken, but they remained important in the 1990s. When Veronica Strang undertook her study, she was told that the "old people" (that is, the long dead ancestors) helped protect the commons by refusing to give resources to strangers. Even for members of the community, it was important to respect the ancestors. Alma Wason told Strang that "Before we catch anything we have to call out to them, to give us some food . . . fish or turtle to catch, and then people start catching something. If you are a stranger and go fishing, you catch nothing, because you don't know how to talk to them, and they don't know you."[46]

The logic of this commons has very little to do with material self-interest. To the indigenous of this part of north

Queensland, the land is alive. It is both father and mother and nurtures all. It is not something to buy or sell or harm. The land is "listening, watching, nurturing, disciplining and balancing human and natural resources."[47] The law of the land is complex and emotional and combines myth with notions of long-term sustainable use. Such a law seems to go beyond the descriptions used by economists to understand human motivation. The relationship between people and commons is personal and not property based.

Misreading the Cultural Commons

It is not enough to see culture as norms that are simply functional to the creation and maintenance of commons. The very debate as to whether commons is functional—that is, whether commons lead to tragedy or triumph—is conditioned by culture. For those who value sustainability, commons is often but not always a source of appropriate sustainability. For those who define economics in terms of accumulation, the commons is more likely to be a failure. From the perspective of commoners, commons are often beneficial, but for elite actors, commons may be seen as failing because they act as a barrier to the growth of their own wealth and power.

Notions of sustainability are also cultural. In some readings, the concept of conservation may even involve an opposition to the commons, with nature being seen as separate from human culture. Rather than looking for ways to use resources sustainably, it is assumed that human beings must be removed from nature and that the metaphor of the "tragedy of the commons" justifies the fencing in of landscapes and the removal of the messy human element. The creation of landscaped country estates in eighteenth-century Britain sometimes meant literally removing villages that distracted from the elite's appreciation of the view of fields and forests untainted by common humanity. The first national parks in the United States assumed a culturally conditioned distinction between culture and nature. The aim was to exclude human actions that might erode "nature" where possible. Colonialism often meant the removal of people from forests as a means of conservation. The global creation of nature reserves and parks during the twentieth century often led to the forced removal of communities living in such areas. Conservation, like economics, can justify enclosure and the defense of elite interests and often led to the criminalization of protests against the loss of usufruct rights. For example, E. P. Thompson's book *Whigs and Hunters* noted that the Black Act made cutting a tree a capital crime in 1723.[48] The "blacks" were groups of hunters who were active in Hampshire and the Windsor Forest and who asserted their customary rights to use forest land that had been enclosed. Suspected of being rebels who supported the Jacobite pretender to the British throne, they were forcefully repressed. The Black Act made fifty supposed crimes—such as cutting a tree or being found in disguise in a forest—into hanging offenses. The deer and other game were "conserved" for the nobility, and poaching remains a crime in Britain in the twenty-first century.

Historical examples seem to illustrate that conservation has been less supported by particular cultural norms, as Elinor Ostrom suggests, than it has been imposed as a way of asserting power. Conservation can be a way of creating what the French sociologist Pierre Bourdieu called cultural capital, which is used to gain social power.[49] Differential access to habitats and hunting has often been a means of establishing and maintaining social distinctions between groups of people. The geographers Paul DeGeorges and Brian Reilly have argued that sub-Saharan Africa is one of the few parts of the planet where humans and mega fauna such as elephants have continued to coexist. Coexistence was threatened by colonial conservation practices when Europeans policed the landscape and expelled rural Africans from conservation areas. Hunters were made into poachers, malnutrition and poverty increased, and Western philosophies of conservation led to bitter disillusionment. This "process continues, previously in the name of conservation and today as 'biodiversity' and ecotourism."[50]

Culture has a destructive side, but it also has had a positive effect on helping different communities to share common ground. The songlines, popularized in Bruce Chatwin's novel of the same name, are a good example of this effect.[51] Indigenous people crossed different territories within Australia by singing songs that guided them through the landscape. These songlines acted as a unique form of navigation, and the right to sing the songlines allowed individuals to move across otherwise hostile territories. These kinds of customary rights have allowed intercommoning with different communities sharing commons. Despite the hostility of local landowners, commons in England were used by traveling gypsy communities and were often traditional sites for boisterous fairs.[52] Commons may work best when they are local with a strong community, but cultural practices have been used to share commons between different and potentially hostile communities. The local and insular bounded commons can be inward-looking and hostile to outsiders, but culture can open doors.

It is also wrong to see commons culture as fixed and unchanging. Christopher Rodgers and his colleagues show how the English commons have been influenced by a medieval and postmedieval notion of "good neighbors" with both formal rules and informal custom allowing different users to profit from the commons. The good-neighbor cultural paradigm was eventually displaced by that of "improvement." In the eighteenth century, this emphasis on agricultural productivity was a part of a cultural shift that led to acceleration in attacks on the commons. In the later nineteenth century, commons were protected through both direct action protests and changes in legislation because they were valued as places of recreation and public landscapes that were associated with the protection of the national heritage. These different ways of framing the commons overlap to some extent, but as E. P. Thompson argues, the English commons were never static, and different groups within a commons battled over rights and meanings within broad cultural frames.[53]

Culture is perhaps innately politically. The French social theorist Michel Foucault's notion of *discourse*, which he derived from the philosopher Friedrich Nietzsche and by which meant "socially situated systems of speech," showed how knowledge is a means of governance. Concepts are used as instruments of power. Thus, although Elinor Ostrom's work on the commons is strong and illuminating, it is not enough to say that commoners are "rational." More fundamentally, Foucault's analysis has been seen as indicating that economics is based on a discourse that allows the exercise of power.[54] Even Adam Smith, often described as the father of economics, seems to nod to this notion, when he observes that "Civil government, so far as it is instituted for the security of property, is, in reality, instituted for the defense of the rich against the poor, or of those who have property against those who have none at all."[55]

We might conclude that culture, in its diverse manifestations from religion to apparently scientific discourse, is to some extent a product of conflict and the different desires of different social groups. In *The Siege of Krishnapur*, the second of his trilogy of novels examining the British empire, one of J. G. Farrell's characters notes that "Culture is a sham. . . . It's a cosmetic painted on life by rich people to conceal its ugliness."[56] From culture, we must turn to discussions of power if we are to better assess the utility of commons as a means of sustaining environmental quality for future generations. This is the subject of chapter 3.

3

Commons in Conflict

All these changes from the original communal property conditions did not, of course, take place without friction, the opposition often taking place in peasants' revolts; hundreds of thousands of these being killed in their attempts to preserve their commons, forests and waters free for all, to re-establish their liberty to hunt, fish and cut wood, and to abolish titles, serfdom and duties.[1]

In early May 1189, the abbot of Crowland closed his fens to the "men of Holland," who used them to pasture their livestock. The abbot's land was intercommoned, which means it was shared by different groups, but the abbot argued that it was his right to restrict access and that custom had established as law the closure of the fens at this time of year to allow the grass to grow lush for summer use. The men of Holland were urged to ignore him by the rival prior of Spalding and refused to remove their animals. In response, the abbot's bailiffs impounded their animals, but the intercommoners entered the marsh and occupied it. Although many local pastures had dried out, which put pressure on the "men of Holland," the abbot claimed that the occupation was at root an act of aggression inspired by greed and envy:

However, the seeming aggressors probably had more reason than is at first apparent from the Crowland tradition. The process of reclamation only gathered pace after the Norman Conquest. It had begun as an essentially communal operation. Before large tracts of the waste were divided up between communities, the whole area had been intercommoned, that is it was used for pasture by all without any boundaries. . . . Elsewhere in the fens Crowland was not slow to take advantage of the opportunities offered to extend their demesnes, and it is probable that they attempted the same around Crowland. The men of Holland's claim was almost certainly based upon their former rights of common in the unenclosed marsh.[2]

The occupiers won, and their intercommoning continued for the time being, despite the hostility of the abbot. The account illustrates the political nature of common-pool property. The historian David Roffe argues that it was within the shift from one kind of commons system to another, with the movement of English society from the Anglo-Saxon to early medieval feudalism:

It was symptomatic of more widespread changes in a society which was moving from a communal and tributary nexus to a seigneurial and manorialized one. There is no reason to doubt that the bounds of Crowland as expressed by the five rivers that surround the island represent some sort of ancient territory.[3]

On January 18, 2012, the English-language versions of *Wikipedia* closed down for a day. Instead of online encyclopedia entries, it showed a black screen with a protest message challenging the Stop Online Piracy Act (SOPA), which was moving through the U.S. legislative system at that time. *Wikipedia* founder Jimmy Wales, along with millions of other users of the Web, argued that far from acting purely against online piracy, SOPA would allow U.S. corporations to close down Websites such as *Wikipedia* merely on the suspicion that links were available to allegedly pirated information. The massive protests against SOPA are part of a wider battle over property rights in cyberspace and over access to the Web commons. Conflict over property rights is a significant issue at present. From free and open-source software to continuing battles over land and seas, the commons is as much about power and politics as it is about issues of culture and management. The Ostrom versus Hardin debate ignores a significant and alarming fact: most commons have not been found to succeed or fail on the basis of their own merits. Instead, they have been enclosed, and access has been restricted and often turned over to purely private ownership or state control. Discussing the assault on the English commons in the eighteenth century, the historian E. P. Thompson notes that "Enclosure (when all the sophistications are allowed for) was a plain enough case of class robbery."[4]

This chapter discusses the often violent destruction of commons by various groups of enclosers as well as resistance by commoners. However, the radical case for commons, which argues that commons work for the benefit of the poor and marginalized, also demands critical attention. A successful commons often involves exclusion so that it can be managed sustainably. Thus, creation of commons does not abolish exploitation. Within systems such as European feudalism and empires such as those of the Aztecs and the Incas, common-pool property may be part of larger structures of hierarchy. Despite being attacked, however, commons still survive. They have continued and been re-created in new forms despite the advance of state and market property relations. Commons is a concept that is both contested and innately political in nature. Power and access to resources remain essential areas for debate.

The Assault on the Commons

Commons have been under attack for centuries. In colonial nations like the United States, Canada, and Australia, indigenous people with communal tenure were increasingly moved to marginal land as European settlers advanced. The assault on the commons has also occurred within Europe. England is a good example of this process. Under the Iron Age tribes and after the Roman conquest, the country remained largely a commons, and commons remained dominant in the Anglo-Saxon period. After the Norman Conquest of 1066, all land was taken under the sovereignty of a foreign monarch, but within this feudal system, peasants had extensive usufruct rights to land so that they could live and reproduce new generations of serfs to work for the lords. Extensive common property-rights systems evolved within this and other forms of European feudalism. After the end of feudalism, commoners initially gained more freedom, but an erosion of usufruct rights took place starting as early the sixteenth century. As the historian Jeanette Neeson notes, enclosure intensified from 1700 to 1820.[5] Karl Marx wrote a detailed account of the enclosure of the commons in Britain in chapter 27 of *Das Kapital*, and his cowriter Friedrich Engels produced a comparative account of the destruction of the commons in Germany.[6] Marx noted that accelerated enclosure in the eighteenth and nineteenth centuries forced peasants from the land and into the cities. A consequence, in his view, was the creation of an urban working class whose members had to work in the formal wage economy because they had been separated from the means of meeting their needs from the land. Marx did not see enclosure as a conspiracy to create a capitalist economy, but he stressed that the destruction of the commons was essential to this kind of society. If individuals could live largely or entirely from common-pool property, they would be unlikely to give up their freedom to become wage laborers. Any work for wages that was undertaken had to be well rewarded because land gave free peasants a strong negotiating position. Only by enclosing the commons could a supply of potential low-wage industrial workers be created.

Marx provided a vivid and instructive example of the clearance of communal clan land in Scotland:

Duchess of Sutherland will suffice here. This person, well instructed in economy, resolved, on entering upon her government, to effect a radical cure, and to turn the whole country, whose population had already been, by earlier processes of the like kind, reduced to 15,000, into a sheep-walk. From 1814 to 1820 these 15,000 inhabitants, about 3,000 families, were systematically hunted and rooted out. All their villages were destroyed and burnt, all their fields turned into pasturage. British soldiers enforced this eviction, and came to blows with the inhabitants. One old woman was burnt to death in the flames of the hut which she refused to leave. Thus this fine lady appropriated 794,000 acres of land that had from time immemorial belonged to the clan. She assigned to the expelled inhabitants about 6,000 acres on the sea-shore—2 acres per family. The 6,000 acres had until this time lain waste, and brought in no income to their owners. The Duchess, in the nobility of her heart, actually went so far as to let these at an average rent of 2s. 6d. per acre to the clansmen, who for centuries had shed their blood for her family. The whole of the stolen clanland she divided into 29 great sheep farms, each inhabited by a single family, for the most part imported English farm-servants. In the year 1835 the 15,000 Gaels were already replaced by 131,000 sheep.[7]

The process of enclosure accelerated in the eighteenth and nineteenth centuries but occurred over a much longer time period. The medieval English commons was already privately owned. Community-controlled commons, without individual ownership, had disappeared by the Norman period in a process that had already been advancing during Anglo-Saxon times. Usufruct rights were eroded over centuries. There has been considerable debate over the nature of enclosure in the eighteenth and nineteenth centuries. A Whig view of history claimed that enclosure was necessary for increased agricultural productivity and has been strongly advocated by some. As the writer Cliff Cobb notes:

Rather than seeing enclosure as a sudden form of expropriation of land rights, it is better understood as one element of a sustained pattern of economic pressure that was associated with agricultural improvement. In some cases, compensation was paid to displaced tenants. In others, their leases expired and were not renewed. The main form of rights that were simply terminated without compensation were foraging rights in the wastelands surrounding villages. For some people in the nineteenth century, the loss of hunting and fishing rights was a matter of life and death. Yet, on the whole, the enclosure of fens and marshes was responsible for an increase in total agricultural output.[8]

The historian Jeanette Neeson challenged this functionalist reading at some length. It is reminiscent of contemporary advocates of enclosure who argue that modernization is necessary and that peasants and indigenous should be displaced to make way for "progress." What is in no doubt is that enclosure in Britain was accompanied by considerable resistance.

From the fourteenth to sixteenth centuries, disputes over enclosure fueled major peasant revolts. A typical example is Kett's rebellion in 1549. It began on June 20 when a landowner fenced in commons at Harpham and Attleborough. In response, local people, who had heard news of enclosure being resisted in Kent, pulled down the fences. For a fortnight, the uprising had no apparent leader until Robert Kett emerged at its head. A neighboring landowner paid peasants to break Kett's fences to distract attention from their own enclosure. Kett joined the peasants in pulling down his own fences. He then led a wider uprising that culminated, before it was put down by German mercenaries and royal troops, in the writing of a manifesto that demanded that King Edward halt enclosure.

The tenor of Kett's speech urging on his peasant army captures something of the revulsion against enclosure in his day:

Now are ye overtopped and trodden down by gentlemen, and put out of possibility ever to recover foot. Rivers of riches ran into the coffers of your landlords, while you are pair'd to the quick, and fed upon pease and oats like beasts. You are fleeced by these landlords for their private benefit, and as well kept under by the public burdens of State wherein while the richer sort favour themselves, ye are gnawn to the very bones. You tyrannous masters often implead, arrest, and cast you into prison, so that they may the more terrify and torture you in your minds, and wind our necks more surely under their arms. And then they palliate these pillories with the fair pretence of law and authority! Fine workmen, I warrant you, are this law and authority, who can do their dealings so closely that men can only discover them for your undoing. Harmless counsels are fit for tame fools; for you who have already stirred there is no hope but in adventuring boldly.[9]

Kett marched on Norwich with an army of 20,000 Norfolk commoners to meet the king, who was holding council in the city. German mercenaries were used to put down the rebellion, and Kett was hung. Resistance continued for centuries, and cataloguing it and assessing its wider causes are too large topics to tackle here. A variety of factors rather than pure opposition to enclosure was apparent. Revolts such as Kett's were also strongly influenced by religion, such as the sixteenth-century conflict between Catholics and Protestants. It is often difficult to separate religion, politics, and ownership as roots of rebellion and war. For example, the Peasant Wars of the sixteenth century in Germany took the form of a religious revolution by the Anabaptists. The right to a communal society was part of their demands, which were fueled both by enclosure and their response to scripture. The Anabaptist leader Thomas Müntzer was captured and under torture confessed that he believed in the heretical notion of *Omnia sunt communia,* which means that "all things are to be held in common."[10]

In Britain, conflict over enclosure and usufruct rights evolved over centuries. As has been noted, the Black Act of 1723 was introduced to repress opponents of enclosure, whose particular grievance was the removal of usufruct rights to gather wood in forests and to hunt game. For centuries, commoners regularly pulled down fences. In a brief history of enclosure in Britain, the environmental activist and writer Simon Fairlie gives an account of resistance to the draining and enclosure of Otmoor in Oxfordshire. The moor was unstinted, which meant that commoners were free to graze cattle and geese during the summer when the wetlands receded. The local Spencer-Churchill family was keen to drain the moor, and advocates of enclosure were dismissive of the commoners: "In looking after a brood of goslings, a few rotten sheep, a skeleton of a cow or a mangy horse, they lost more than they might have gained by their day's work, and acquired habits of idleness and dissipation, and a dislike to honest labor, which has rendered them the riotous and lawless set of men that they have now shown themselves to be."[11]

In aiming to improve land, enclosure has major environmental effects. Habitats may be degraded as farm yields increase. Fairlie notes that opposition to the draining of Otmoor was fierce, but the effects in raising agricultural productivity were initially disappointing:

The first proposal to drain and enclose the land in 1801, by the Spencer Churchills, was staved off by armed mobs who appeared every time the authorities tried to pin up enclosure notices. A second attempt in 1814 was again met with "large mobs armed with every description of offensive weapon."

The enclosure and drainage was eventually forced through over the next few years, but it failed to result in any immediate agricultural benefit. A writer in another local paper judged: "instead of expected improvement in the quality of the soil, it had been rendered almost totaly worthless . . . few crops yielding any more than barely sufficient to pay for labour and seed."

In 1830, 22 farmers were acquitted of destroying embankments associated with the drainage works, and a few weeks later, heartened by this result, a mob gathered and perambulated the entire commons pulling down all the fences. Lord Churchill arrived with a troop of yeomen, arrested 44 of the rioters and took them off to Oxford gaol in a paddy wagon.

Now it happened to be the day of St Giles' fair, and the street of St Giles along which the yeomanry brought their prisoners, was crowded. The men in the wagons raised the cry "Otmoor forever," the crowd took it up, and attacked the yeomen with great violence, hurling brickbats, stones and sticks at them from every side . . . and all 44 prisoners escaped.[12]

Similar tales of fence destruction and opposition to enclosure from across the British Isles span the entire period from the fourteenth century up until the late nineteenth. They can be paralleled in other European countries. What has been largely ignored in the social history is the environmental impact of enclosure. Exclusion of peasants from woodland, the drainage of marshland, and the shift to more intensive forms of agriculture have led to environmental change. Not all of the changes have been negative. The signature British hedge was an instrument of enclosure, a physical reminder of the destruction of the commons in the landscape. Although the hedges made the commoners landless, they also provide a habitat for many birds and small mammals.

Enclosure and Colonization

Enclosure in Europe helped fuel enclosure in European colonies. "Excess" populations cleared from the land were resettled in North America, Latin America, New Zealand, Australia, and other territories. Former commoners from Europe were resettled onto land that had been the common-pool property of indigenous peoples across the planet. Thus, the destruction of the English commons used their enclosure to create new private property. For example, the story of how the indigenous of North America, who practiced varied forms of commons ownership, were pushed from their territories is a long and bloody one. Even where accompanied by legal means, this practice was ethically dubious. Indigenous people often had no conception of purely private property and did not realize that they were transferring ownership. William Cronon notes how territory was sold by indigenous peoples, who believed that they had allowed only usufruct rights (such as hunting) to land and not its outright alienation and enclosure.[13]

Indigenous populations were relocated to ever shrinking territories as their lands were taken in wars of conquest that swept across North America. As has been noted, the colonists argued, with reference to the philosopher John Locke, that those who worked the land should enjoy the fruits of their labor. Because they claimed that the indigenous commons did not lead to the productive exploitation of the land, they felt that such landscould be taken and turned into private property that would bring forth real wealth.

Violence was not the only means of converting indigenous commons into private property, but it played a part, as it did in the Pequot War of 1634 to 1638. The Pequot, who survived epidemics brought by settlers better than many other New England tribes, nonetheless lost their independence during this conflict. A local dispute led members of a client tribe of the Pequot to kill a colonial smuggler and slaver named John Stone. As a result and with indigenous allies, the colonists attacked the Pequot with a ferocity that was not known in previous inter-indigenous wars. The Mystic massacre of Pequot broke the tribe. Some of those who survived joined tribes to the east and the south, and others were sold as slaves. Victory was seen as the judgment of God by the colonists: "Let the whole Earth be filled with his Glory! Thus the LORD was pleased to smite our Enemies in the hinder Parts, and to give us their Land for an Inheritance."[14] The violence of the war led to further erosion of tribal lands in New England as other indigenous groups were reluctant to oppose colonial advances because of the fear of possible extinction.

The evolving United States of America often claimed that indigenous land rights were to be protected. For example, the U.S. Congress's 1789 Northwest Ordinance, which ultimately opened land to the northwest of the Ohio River to colonial settlement, stated that "The utmost good faith shall always be observed toward the Indian; their land property shall never be taken from them without their consent; and in their property, rights, and liberty, they shall never be invaded or disturbed."[15]

However, the land was taken by force. A coalition of tribes counterattacked and were victorious against the U.S. Army, but despite this initial victory, they were defeated at the Battle of Fallen Timbers by General Wayne in 1794. This defeat opened up much of what is now Ohio and Indiana to white settlers.

The process continued right up to the start of the twentieth century. Colonial advances, indigenous counterattacks, and the gradual hegemony of settlers and the transformation of land ownership from commons to private property swept North America. Religious justification and Locke's views on property were used to make land seizure legitimate, but conservation in more recent times has also played a role. In the nineteenth century, national parks were created that excluded the common rights of the indigenous. As the environmental historian William Cronon notes:

> To this day, for instance, the Blackfeet continue to be accused of "poaching" on the lands of Glacier National Park that originally belonged to them and that were ceded by treaty only with the proviso that they be permitted to hunt there.
> The removal of Indians to create an "uninhabited wilderness"—uninhabited as never before in the human history of the place—reminds us just how invented, just how constructed, the American wilderness really is. To return to my opening argument: there is nothing natural about the concept of wilderness. It is entirely a creation of the culture that holds it dear, a product of the very history it seeks to deny. Indeed, one of the most striking proofs of the cultural invention of wilderness is its thoroughgoing erasure of the history from which it sprang. In virtually all of its manifestations, wilderness represents a flight from history.[16]

To return to an earlier discussion, William Cronon's observation shows that culture can be used as a weapon to erase the commons. Cultural norms are shaped by the exercise of power and, in turn, can be instruments of coercion or at least a support for coercive action. Colonial commons were created. The Boston Common is one example of many, but these were often enclosed in a society that believed private property was superior. One commons that did endure until 1904 was the chestnut commons of the southern Appalachian Mountains. Here local people gathered chestnuts and allowed their pigs to roam the woodland. Oral history shows that the commons was seen to provide "Manna from heaven" in the form of nutritious food for the poor. These commons came under attack:

The closure of the commons in southwestern Virginia Blue Ridge counties, and perhaps in other Appalachian mountain counties, followed a very different path from that of much of the South. Following the Civil War, many interests worked to close the commons. People who wanted to constrain the liberties of formerly enslaved African Americans, large landowners who wanted to protect their property rights, mercantile interests, and even railroads companies concerned about liability when trains killed livestock tried to pass laws requiring farmers to fence in their livestock. They encountered considerable resistance on the part of small farmers and others, particular in mountain communities. However, through persistence, political skill, and skullduggery they often succeeded.[17]

Other chestnut commons were eventually wrecked by the blight, which destroyed the trees after 1904, rather than such plots and plans.

In Latin America, commons were virtually universal and very diverse. Empires like those of the Incas and Aztecs were politically sophisticated, economically robust and based upon common ownership of the land. The basic unit of the Inca economy was the *ayllu*. The *ayllu* was composed of land used by a collection of families producing in common, a third of produce went to the empire, a third to the religious organizations and a third was retained by the community. A vast empire rested on communal property, suggesting that accumulation was possible, under a system of common but not entirely equal production and distribution. The *ayllu* system was eroded but far from eliminated by the Spanish invasion, and struggles over land and land rights have continued to shape Peruvian history. To prevent overuse Inca village communities owned particular patches of ocean, in common, rather than allowing a free for all.[18]

Colonial enclosure is a feature of the Americas and of all the parts of the world where European empires were constructed, including Africa, India, Australia, New Zealand, and much of Asia. In Tasmania, for example, a sophisticated system of land rights that utilized selective burning to create a more ecologically diverse and productive landscape was destroyed by European invasion.[19] In what is now Australia, direct capture of land was achieved by military force, cultural values were used to justify such force, and law was used to create new property-rights systems. The spread of diseases also weakened indigenous societies. The construction of market-based economies tended to integrate communal populations and promote self-enclosure. It became less and less easy to gain access to commons for animal grazing, hunting, and gathering wood for fuel. This intensified the need to buy and sell in the market rather than depending on local commons, and this accelerated more intensive use of existing commons to generate surpluses for exchange. More intensive use of existing common-pool property, in turn, disrupted traditional forms of management, creating "tragedies" that were used to justify greater enclosure.

Indigenous peoples often have been relocated to land that was seen as marginal, especially in terms of agricultural use. Many indigenous groups are now forest dwellers, but they often are the remnants of nonforest peoples who were pushed into new land. In the twenty-first century, previously marginal areas are often sought for oil, gas, mineral, and metal exploration, which puts pressure on existing commons and commons-based peoples. The effects on sustainable environmental management are often serious.

Assaults on the commons continue, often justified with reference to notions of development and progress. In Peru, for example, Amazon-dwelling communities organized into AIDESEP, a confederation of different indigenous groups that are committed to sustainable development, came into conflict with the Peruvian government over plans to open up the rainforest for exploration by gas and oil companies. The results of such proposals accelerate climate change both by extracting fossil fuels and by degrading the Amazon, which acts as a carbon sink. Indigenous people argue that such plans for fossil-fuel extraction threaten their own economic activity based on sustainable use of the forests. AIDESEP used nonviolent direct action to halt the granting of concessions to companies, but at Bagua on June 5, 2009, World Environment Day, the militarized Peruvian police killed many indigenous protesters. In the aftermath of the killings, Peruvian president Alan García compared AIDESEP to a dog who refused to give up a bone, even though it was not gnawing it but merely jealous of others who would gain nourishment from it. He argued that the indigenous failed to make full use of the resources of the rainforest and prevented Peru from developing: "There is a conspiracy aimed at stopping us from using our natural resources for the good, growth and quality of life of our people."[20]

Perhaps the commons is never pure. It certainly has coexisted with repressive political systems and other forms of more exclusive property. Nonetheless, the global assault on the commons did real damage to formerly communal peoples, and such attacks on indigenous people and commons continue in the twenty-first century. Across continents, colonialism and marketization helped to eliminate usufruct rights and exclude people. The story with some variations is near universal.

Ecological Imperialism

For environmental historian Alfred Crosby, the concept of *Ecological Imperialism: The Biological Expansion of Europe, 900–1900* is part of the story of the commons and enclosure on a planetary scale. He notes that European colonialism directly oppressed peoples across the world and reshaped nonhuman nature. European settlers, both deliberately and accidentally, introduced new species to the Americas and other parts of the world. The environment was radically altered, for example, by rabbits that were taken to Australia and then reduced vegetation growth.[21] Madhav Gadgil and Ramachandra Guha note that sustainable local economies, based on commons and usufruct rights, were often swept away.[22] "Tragedy of the commons" type arguments were used by the British in India to object to commons regimes and to justify the formalizing of property rights. The deeper motive was to reengineer the environment to meet the needs of an imperial economy. Forests typically were enclosed, often were logged, and usually replaced with monocultures. This boosted short-term economic production but reduced biodiversity with negative environmental consequences.

European colonization of North America was also destructive of wildlife and reduced biodiversity. One notes the disappearance of the passenger pigeon and the buffalo. "Nature" was tamed by private property and exploited intensively to fuel the imperial project. Previous indigenous forms of land management had transformed nature, shaping it for human needs and sometimes causing extinction, but colonialism led to a major reduction in biodiversity.

From Vietnam to South Africa, New Zealand to Alaska, the erosion of commons and customary rights oppressed non-European human populations and also had a drastic effect on the wider environment. Implicit in the radical case for commons, which is critically discussed in the next section, is the notion that commons free both human beings and other species. Marx quoted the German Anabaptist revolutionary Thomas Müntzer, who suggested "that all creatures have been turned into property, the fishes in the water, the birds in the air, the plants on the earth; the creatures, too, must become free."[23]

The nineteenth-century British poet John Clare wrote numerous verses about the enclosure of the commons. Like Müntzer, he linked the fencing of land to the dispossession of peasants like himself but also of other species, noting in his verses the loss to rabbits and bees of the formerly free land. He condemned an agriculture that was based on productive growth that squeezed the poor and the animals. E. P. Thompson notes that "Clare may be described, without hindsight, as a poet of ecological protest: he was not writing about man here and nature there, but lamenting a threatened equilibrium in which both were involved."[24] In *The Mores*, Clare mourned the conversion of the communal moor into enclosed private property, with ill effects both for peasants sent to the workhouse because they could no longer subsist from the land and for creatures who were restricted by profit-oriented farming. The plover vanished along "with commons wild & gay."[25] The literary theorist Ronald Paul suggests that for Clare, "the privatization of the common land appears in itself as unnatural, as a crime against the animals, birds, insects, trees, flowers, rivers and streams themselves."[26] Such sentiments suggest that the enclosure of the commons is intimately connected with the creation of an economic system that degraded the environment and reduced biodiversity. From this perspective, the landscape becomes a factory, and nature is sweated to produce more value.

The Radical Case for the Commons

If the Ostrom and Hardin debate focuses on the rationality and economic value of commons, another tradition of commons discourse might be termed the radical case for commons. There is a tradition of looking at commons within a historical context as a source of revolutionary political energy. This school of thought is well represented in Europe by British Marxist historians such as E. P. Thompson and Christopher Hill. It is also significant in Latin America.

The commons can be linked to Marx's espousal of a system of communism that is based on the withering away of forms of ownership based on both state and private property. From discussing efficient management of resources to promoting overlapping ideologies of revolution is quite a step. The right to commons remains a demand of radical social movements in the twenty-first century, peasants still campaign for common land, and hackers fight for cyberspace without walls.

As has been noted, the English folk tradition saw peasants struggling for communal land rights in resistance to both feudal and market-based systems. By allowing peasants the means of reproduction, the commons was vital in sustaining feudalism. Common-pool property was part of an oppressive system, but peasants nonetheless recognized their material interests in seeking to preserve or extend the commons. The historian Peter Linebaugh examines this struggle closely in his book *Magna Carta Manifesto: Liberties and Commons for All*. He notes that the Magna Carta of 1215 was accompanied by a forest charter that gave commoners clear and strong rights to use forests. Linebaugh argues that the rebellion against King John saw commoners move in alliance with the barons against an unpopular monarch. Although the Magna Carta has been seen as maintaining private property rights, the struggle for commons was essential to this rebellion. Linebaugh argues that commoners had a tradition of defense of the commons and opposed Norman rule when in 1066 William I introduced the feudal system. Thus, he observes that chapter 47 of the Magna Carta "disafforested" areas of new royal forest that had been created in King John's reign. *Forest* means controlled and enclosed from commoners, so rather than implying that woods were to be cut down, it meant that they were to be restored to the people. Chapter 48 sought to remove restrictions on the woodland commons that were important to many commoners. "Evil customs" imposed by sheriffs and other officials on commoners were to be "utterly abolished by them so as never to be restored."[27] Later, when they no longer needed peasant support, having won their battle against the monarch, the barons sought to extend enclosure.

Peasant rebellions in England in the next four centuries, as has been noted, were focused largely on opposition to the enclosure of commons. Typically, during the 1381 peasant revolt, peasants pulled down fences to restore land that had been enclosed in Winchester and Cambridge.

During the 1640s, the Diggers, who can be seen as the extreme left of the Levellers, who in turn were radical opponents of the monarchy during the Civil War, argued that commons were vital to political and economic regeneration. They occupied land at St. Georges Hill in Surrey and tried to grow food during a period of rising inflation. They eventually were removed by local landowners but attempted to create new communal settlements across England. The ideological roots of the Diggers in an era of extreme political turmoil are complex, but their radical defense of the commons is clear.

They used the Bible to present their views, noting that

The Earth (which was made to be a Common Treasury of relief for all, both Beasts and Men) was hedged in to In-closures by the teachers and rulers, and the others were made Servants and Slaves: And that Earth that is within this Creation made a Common Store-house for all, is bought and sold, and kept in the hands of a few, whereby the great Creator is mightily dishonored, as if he were a respector of persons, delighting in the comfortable Livelihood of some, and rejoycing in the miserable povertie and straits of others. From the beginning it was not so.

Their reference to mother earth—"one that is born in the Land, may be fed by the Earth his Mother"—perhaps surprisingly echoes indigenous commons discourse.[28]

In his book written with Marcus Rediker, *The Many-Headed Hydra: Sailors, Slaves, Commoners, and the Hidden History of the Revolutionary Atlantic*, Peter Linebaugh has argued that there were connections between the British radical commons tradition, indigenous land rights, and slave rebellions Escaped slaves like the Maroons in Jamaica created their own commons, and radical Europeans joined indigenous commons in North America.[29] Radical commons discourse was also utilized by rebels in Australia.[30] The French philosopher Jean-Jacques Rousseau also expressed a radical commons sentiment claiming that first individual to enclose property and take it invented evil.[31] The radical philosophers Michael Hardt and Antonio Negri argued that "The commons is the incarnation, the production, and the liberation of the multitude."[32]

In Latin America, indigenous struggles to defend the commons have helped shape the structure of political and social change. In the twenty-first century, leftist leaders like Evo Morales in Bolivia have specified the need to restore commons in opposition to capitalism as part of a project of ecological restoration. The need to defend commons has been central to indigenous struggles in Bolivia and also in a number of Latin American countries including Peru, Ecuador, and Chile. Indigenous advocacy of commons has increasingly affected the political system. The Bolivian academic Félix Patzi Paco looked to the Inca *ayllu*, which was a communal form of land ownership and economic activity, as an inspiration for his book *Tercer Sistema: Modelo comunal: Propuesta alternative aparasalir del capitalismo y del socialismo*, which translates as "A third system, the communal model: Proposals for an alternative to capitalism and socialism."[33]

The case that commons is always oppositional to capitalism and empire seems secure, and if unthinking economic accumulation together with environmental degradation follows the destruction of commons, then their restoration may be seen as vital to a sustainable future. However, the "radical" case for the commons can be criticized and not just by those who dismiss the wishes of the commoners to graze their cattle and gather firewood and medicinal plants.

Conflicted Commons

To the extent that we can ever talk about established historical facts, we have come some considerable distance from Garrett Hardin's "tragedy of the commons" thesis. The open-access commons can lead to tragedy, but commons normally are managed and productive within broad ecological constraints. The real tragedy has been the often bloody enclosure and destruction of the commons. However, the radical case for commons as a basis for an egalitarian and ecologically sustainable society does demand critical examination. The commons is not utopia. Common-pool property rights do not guarantee a free and equal society. Commons may have inspired Marx's love of communism, but commons may be less equal and free than has sometimes been suggested.

There are a number of reasons that commons, even without the violent threat of enclosure, are not necessarily egalitarian and do not necessarily work without conflict. The commons identified by Elinor Ostrom paradoxically function because of fences. Her research indicates that well-managed commons may require external barriers. Enclosure normally is seen as the abolition of commons, but Elinor Ostrom argues that commons may often be difficult to sustain without enclosure. To maintain commons, stints and usufruct rules are often put in place. Those who have the right to use the commons will agree to, say, the number of animals they can graze or days they can catch fish in a season. These agreed stints prevent overuse, but individuals who lack commons rights generally must be excluded to prevent overexploitation. A revisionist historical criticism of the radical commons approach that was put forward by the historian Ben Maddison suggests that in some circumstances a community may exclude marginalized or poorer groups from accessing resources.[34] Commons often rely on usufruct rights, which provide access to use without ownership of land. Because in the twenty-first century we are familiar with private property, such rights may be forgotten easily. Private property can be used, despite some legal restrictions, more or less in whatever way an owner sees fit; therefore, usufruct rules may be invisible. In any commons, however, users are likely to have particular rights to use the commons in particular ways rather than enjoying unlimited free access. The right simply to walk across a common is different from the right to gather fallen wood. The right to graze one's geese is different from the right to build a hut or grow carrots. With rights come power relations. Property can be seen as a power relationship. Commons is rarely the absence of property, common property is not intrinsically equal, and some users may have more rights than others. Commons can involve hierarchy.

Commons rights, as has been shown, are not simply associated with communally owned property. An individual may hold a title to land, but in a commons system such apparently "private ownership" is accompanied by usufruct rights for others. Marx's essay on the law of the woods examined how commoners had customary rights to pick fallen wood in a forest owned by the local nobility. In this case, common rights were destroyed when commoners were excluded and arrested for stealing the wood. Although the commons existed, the woodland was still owned by an elite social class.

One of the best examples of commons, which inspired Elinor Ostrom's work, was the Törbel grazing ground in Switzerland. This commons worked within a relatively equal society without feudal rulers, but it was inspired by practical considerations rather than ideological concerns. It was a straightforward example of a situation where entirely private ownership would have been impractical because farmers needed both winter and summer pastures for their herds. Private ownership of fields some distance apart would have been far from ideal, and the land that was appropriate for farming cattle shifted and changed with the seasons. Commons rights simply made it easier to farm. These grazing commons were integrated into a wider commons economy, but this was far from communism and instead was part of a market economy. Eighty percent of grazing in Switzerland is based on a diversity of different commons in the twenty-first century, but Switzerland is far from being a radically egalitarian society or one transitioning away from capitalism.

In some circumstances, commons may be the basis of a more equal society, but commons can coexist within a number of far from egalitarian societies. There are numerous cases of commons being part of imperial property. Medieval Britain might be seen as a golden age of the commons, but all property was owned ultimately by the monarch. Within this feudal system, property was owned via a chain or ladder, and feudal lords in localities had control. Commons were often made up of marginal land, while the most fertile ground was reserved for production for the benefit of those in power. As noted, commons were worked by the serfs so that they could maintain themselves by receiving enough food and firewood to reproduce future generations, who would continue to work the land for their masters. In this example of feudalism, commons had vital functions within a society that was based on extreme inequality, militarism, and conquest.

Different societies with different systems of communal ownership can come into conflict. In Latin America, common property was dominant. Such dominance included the existence of common-pool property systems within the Aztec and Inca empires. These were also unequal societies that were highly militaristic and certainly expansionary. Both Aztec and Inca political systems sought to invade and absorb other societies that practiced communal ownership. Such expansion illustrates that different commons-based political systems can be violently antagonistic.

As a relatively egalitarian and potentially ecological means of managing resources, the commons has strong virtues, but the radical case for commons is far from pure. Commons does not dissolve conflict. Even when managed consensually, commons function generally with some form of exclusion. To repeat our argument, rights have to be established, and such creation of rights is intrinsically bound up with questions of power. When charting the erosion of commons, there is a danger of seeing commons as homogeneous, but commons have changed throughout human history. They have not taken a simple form in a given society. Again, this reflects critically on Elinor Ostrom's account, which tends to assume a broad evolutionary functionalism—that is, commons develop in ways that make them most economically efficiently. In reality, political struggles over power establish territory and the rules that govern the use of such territory, even within forms of collective ownership. Commons do not abolish conflict and, in a particular sense, will always be contested.

Even local commons existing today in the United Kingdom show that commons can involve exclusion: one group's usufruct rights may exclude others. The following news story appeared on the BBC Website in 2011:

People from a private Berkshire estate who have historic rights to pick watercress say their river is being targeted by thieves.

Two women walking near Hungerford saw a woman and two younger men in the River Dun fishing and filling six large plastic dustbin liners with watercress.

People who live in 100 houses in High Street, Church Street and Bridge Street in Hungerford are known as "commoners."

They have shooting, grazing and fishing rights under centuries-old laws.

It is illegal for others to pick watercress on the estate.

Robert James, Trustee and Honorary Secretary of the Town and Manor of Hungerford, said: "Two ladies who were walking up Freeman's Marsh saw these people were in the river.

"They had black plastic sacks and they were filling them with watercress.

"I had a call at home, so I got in my car and drove off to apprehend them, with two police officers."

However, by the time Mr James and the police reached the river the group of three were no longer there.

The River Dun is a tributary of the River Kennet. Both rivers are included in the watercress rights of commoners.

While land owned by the manor and town is out of bounds to foragers, West Berkshire Council allows people to pick fruit and vegetables on its own land.

Council spokesman Keith Ulyatt said "In the true spirit of the countryside, anyone is free to come and pick blackberries, apples and so on from any council-owned countryside land."[35]

The common can be associated with conservative sentiments that are rooted in tradition and custom. Far from wanting revolution, its users may be conservatives rather than radicals. The poet John Clare is a good example. Many of his poems, as has been noted, celebrate the beauty of the commons and mourn attacks on both the poor and nonhuman nature. However, he combined love of commons with a patriotic affection for king and country, arguing that "I am as far as my politics reaches 'King and Country'—no Innovations in Religion and Government say I."[36] The social movement theorist Charles Tilly noted that disruptive and militant direct action in sixteenth- to eighteenth-century England might be combined with deferential appeals to elite actors such as the monarch or local nobles.[37]

Thus, it is easy to oversimplify the historical record and see a period of enclosure that put an end to a harmonious and largely egalitarian form of property ownership. Different groups within common-pool property systems may have different interests. Christopher Rodgers and his colleagues note that diverse usufruct rights may give rise to conflict if they are not carefully managed. For example, turbary, which is the right to dig peat, may infringe on grazing rights. Some commoners might want to gather bracken or other vegetation for domestic use, but this can be to the detriment of herders. In England for many centuries, commons were managed in a legal sense by manorial courts. The lord of the manor and peasant users would tend to have different interests in the commons. Rodgers and his colleagues also note how elite landowners in more recent times have tried to retain moors for grouse hunting and to reduce the rights of those who prefer them for grazing. Recent legislation on land use in the United Kingdom has given more public access to those who wish to use commons for walking and other forms of recreation, despite the wishes of owners who might prefer to keep access closed so they can hunt.

E. P. Thompson argues that far from being an exception, conflicts over common rights were the norm. As early as the thirteenth century, common rights "were exercised according to 'time-hallowed custom,' but they were being disputed in time-hallowed ways. Conflict over 'botes' or 'estover' (small wood for fencing, repair of buildings, fuel) or 'turbary' . . . was never ending."[38]

Any commons can involve a power relationship that excludes noncommoners, something that can be forgotten by radical advocates of the commons. Commons often exclude those seen as outsiders, and defining some individuals as commoners who are part of a community and others who are not part of that community is a political question. Although intercommoning can also exist with shared commons, conflict is perhaps intrinsic to the very concept of communal ownership.

Commons, Conflict, and Gender

Gender relations can be forgotten when examining the history of commons. Commons have worked to the exclusion of particular groups in society, including women, but it can also be argued that women have lost more with enclosure than men have. There also are many examples of women who organized to fight enclosure and defend the commons. Commons cannot be isolated from the wider effects produced by the social systems within which they are found, and commons in societies that marginalize women will tend to reproduce such marginalization.

The historian Jane Humphries has argued that women's domestic labor in peasant societies is often relatively invisible to historians.[39] The economic value produced by commons is often not measured in money terms, whereas the value produced by enclosure is more likely to be so. Because women in peasant and indigenous societies have gathered and gleaned more often as part of an informal economy than as part of a monetized one, enclosure of the commons therefore reduced women's access to a vital part of their domestic economy. The feminist historian and autonomist Marxist Silvia Federici suggests that male commoners found it easier than women to survive attacks on European commons in the sixteenth and seventeenth centuries. She argues that women suffered the most because when access to land was lost and communities destroyed, they found it more difficult than men to move away and start again. Women were less mobile because of pregnancies and childcare, they could not become soldiers for pay, and although some accompanied armies as cooks, servants, prostitutes, or wives, by the seventeenth century this option disappeared as armies became more regimented and the crowds of women that used to follow them were removed from battlefields.[40]

Commons cannot, however, be seen as automatically female-friendly institutions. In fact, women may have a more marginal position in systems of usufruct than some men do. Most commons, as has been discussed, are managed, and different social groups may have different rights of access and use. Indian commons often gave more rights to higher-caste individuals, and lower-caste members of society, particularly poorer women, have had less access to them and less control over how they are managed.

Nonetheless, women have often been at the forefront of struggles to defend the commons. Women have often taken militant action, including breaking fences and demolishing hedges, to restore commons. Plumstead Common in South London, which remains greenspace in the present century, was apparently rescued by angry women in the nineteenth century:

On a Saturday in May 1870, "a number of the lower class, who were resolved to test their rights" demolished fences and carried off the wood. "A party of women, armed with saws and hatchets, first commenced operations by sawing down a fence enclosing a meadow adjoining the residence of Mr Hughes." Fences belonging to William Tongue were pulled down. There was talk of pulling down Hughes' house as well. Hughes called the coppers, and some nickings followed. The next day 100s of people gathered and attacked fences put up by a Mr Jeans. When the bobbies arrived many vandals took refuge in the local pubs.[41]

Women may have particularly valued usufruct rights to gather fruit and fuel from forests and other commons and continue to fight for them. This struggle is again reflected in examples of indigenous opposition to the removal of usufruct rights to make way for oil and gas exploration. When Salomon Awanash Wajush, an indigenous leader, was asked by Peru's *La República* newspaper why she defended the Amazon rainforests, she replied, "The jungle is our mother, our pharmacy, our supermarket, our home."[42]

Continuing Commons

Whether via Garrett Hardin or the more simplistic readings of Karl Marx, common-pool property can seem like a relic of a romantic or wrecked past or a mixture of both. The commons belong to prehistoric peoples, medieval English peasants, and the Russian mir of the nineteenth century, all swept away by the forces of capitalism and progress. However, there is considerable evidence that the commons is not a product of a particular stage in an oversimplification of human history. The commons have been under assault for hundreds of years but have never been obliterated and are continuing to grow back.

E. P. Thompson's detailed research into the commons of England shows that there was considerable resistance to the erosion of the commons. Although such resistance was often defeated (for example, when enclosures gained parliamentary approval, particularly in the eighteenth and nineteenth centuries), resistance did not always fail. Thompson notes that protest by commoners preserved virtually all the parks and greenspaces that can be found in modern London. Commons in such diverse localities as Mongolia, the Peruvian Amazon, and much of India remain because of similar militant defense.

Around 500,000 hectares of common land remain in England and Wales. The English commons are privately owned, but access rights have been strengthened in recent decades, both for lowland commons, which are used mainly for recreation, and upland commons that retain an agricultural role, particularly for grazing livestock.[43]

Commons does not cover just land and seas. As the autonomist academic Massimo de Angelis argues, alternatives to private-property relations may take a myriad of forms and perhaps can never quite be defeated, even within systems that are largely hostile to collective ownership. He argues that "it is important to emphasize not only that enclosures happen all the time, but also that there is constant commoning." He suggests that people should try to create resources and access them outside market relationships based on private property and buying and selling.[44] Where there is potential for ownership, there is often potential for common-pool property arrangements. Commons dominates cyberspace, as has been shown. The World Wide Web is essentially a commons. The production of free or open-source software is also a significant example of common-property production. Debates over copyright have been used to extend the concept of commons. One relevant concept is that of *copyleft*, where in contrast to copyright, creative work can be copied and used by others as long as it is not sold for profit. Richard Stallman has developed such licenses.

Property rights involve the exercise of power, and those individuals or groups who write the law have power. The historian Malcolm Chase notes that the *Poor Man's Guardian*, a radical newspaper, observed in 1835 that property "is but the creation of law. Whoever makes the law has the power of appropriating the national wealth. If they did not make the law, they would not have the property."[45] The historical record of conflict over common-pool property rights continues to be played out in new arenas. The music industry remains one area where this is evident, as is illustrated by the emergence of sampling in hip-hop and electronic music in the 1980s. One of the earliest samples is an accelerated drum beat called the "Amen break." It is six seconds of a drum solo by Gregory Coleman from The Winstons' 1969 funk record called "Amen, Brother." The Winstons have never received a cent from the musicians and DJs who have sampled the beat in hundreds of songs since the 1980s. The Winstons, in turn, based the drum solo on a previous piece of music. In his video essay "Can I Get an Amen?,"

Free and open-source advocate Nathan Harrison looks at the Amen break as a form of commons and its appropriation as a form of communing. He observes that hip-hop music grew in the 1980s and 1990s by imaginative sampling. According to Harrison, The Winstons saw their beat borrowed for free, but later a company copyrighted the Amen break and made it illegal to use without paying a fee. Harrison argues that creativity is stifled by such enclosure. The Amen break example illustrates that commons, communing, and enclosure are perhaps constant processes.[46]

Processes of enclosure continue and do not just cause injustice to users as the Amen break example shows but may threaten our future as a species. Enclosure is associated with the degradation of the environment historically but also in the present. To create a sustainable future, we need to halt destructive enclosure and find ways to manage property at all levels, from the local to the global, to balance ecological realities with continued prosperity.

How can the examination of commons help us to frame questions about how we can be good ancestors, rather than greedy and abusive parents, of future generations? And how can environmental historians best learn more about the nature of commons in the past to inform further discussion of a sustainable future? These questions are discussed in the final chapter of this book.

4

Questions for Good Ancestors

In March 2005, the Onondaga Nation of Indians filed suit against the state of New York and several large corporate polluters that had done business in the vicinity of Syracuse. In their complaint, the Onondagas said that they were "one with the land and consider themselves stewards of it. It is the duty of the Nation's leaders to work for a healing of this land, to protect it, and to pass it on to future generations." The state and the corporate polluters, they claimed, must undo the damage that they had done to the Onondagas' traditional homeland, especially to Onondaga Lake, the site of the founding of the Iroquois League in myth and memory. The Onondagas, in short, brought a land claim not to drive New Yorkers out of their homes, as some feared that they might, or to gain leverage to acquire a casino but "in the hope that it may hasten the process of reconciliation and bring lasting justice, peace, and respect among all who inhabit this area."[1]

Jared Diamond's *Collapse: How Societies Choose to Fail or Survive* is a bestselling environmental history book. Although not an academic work, it is well referenced and draws widely on the historical literature. Diamond, a geography professor who is known for his books on popular science, uses historical examples of societies that he suggests have collapsed due to environmental factors to argue that we should learn from history to take better care of our environment. It is difficult to summarize *Collapse*, but it does illustrate some of the difficulties of using the past to guide future sustainable practice. Among the historical examples that Diamond examines, the most controversial has been Easter Island. He argues that historical and archeological evidence suggests that the once lushly forested but remote Pacific Island was wrecked by overexploitation: "I have often asked myself, 'What did the Easter Islander who cut down the last palm tree say while he was doing it?,'" suggesting that the islanders might argue that technology would save them or the "market" would rescue their environment and society from disaster.[2]

Jared Diamond's conclusions have been debated at some length. His argument that the islanders were living in poverty when Europeans arrived has been challenged. It has even been suggested that the deforestation may have been a result of the introduction of rats rather than through thoughtless overfelling.[3] His suggestion that islanders were so affected by self-induced environmental catastrophe that they resorted to cannibalism has been strongly criticized. The debates around Easter Island's environment are complex, and European incursions reduced the preexisting population even after the supposed collapse. Causation is problematic: if the island suffered degradation, was this self-induced, and did it lead to political collapse? Or did a failure of political institutions lead to less effective environmental management, which caused deforestation? Diamond should be commended for drawing attention to environmental problems in the past, and he does briefly address the question of commons. He also illustrates that environmental history is more than a parable of destruction. Environmental sustainability introduces complex questions, and the past can help to answer them but does not automatically produce answers.

The word *history* implies a story, and the stories that historians tell can condition the ways they research history. Narrative frames influence the questions asked and help to shape the conclusions made. This book is conditioned by a narrative, too—a story of effective commons management and the enclosure of the commons by the rich and powerful. Environmental sustainability has been treated using other narratives, such as the notion that degradation is an inevitable result of growing population and exploitation. Garrett Hardin's "tragedy of the commons" is part of this view and is developed in his notion of "lifeboat ethics." Hardin argues that on a small lifeboat (such as the small planet Earth), unless some passengers are thrown overboard, the boat will sink and all will be drowned. Vicious exclusion is compassionate because compassion for all would mean extinction. Thomas Malthus, the early nineteenth-century economist, argued that overpopulation would lead to disaster, and Hardin's criticism of the commons was strongly linked to this concern that humans cannot control their numbers. A narrative of technological optimism that has been termed *cornucopianism* counters this rather bleak Malthusianism. This approach assumes that market forces and scientific developments will allow more growth and sustained exploitation of the environment, averting disaster. One of Jared Diamond's critics, the anthropologist Benny Peiser, is a strong advocate of such an approach, suggesting that environmental concerns are often exaggerated.[4] Cornucopians, in contrast to Malthusians, argue that environmental problems have been overcome throughout history by markets, technological advances, and human ingenuity and that a laissez-faire approach therefore remains best. Such an approach can be argued statistically, as the Danish writer Bjørn Lomborg attempts in *The Skeptical Environmentalist: Measuring the Real State of the World*, where he suggests that data indicate that environmental quality is improving rather than degrading on a global scale.[5] The economist Wilfred Beckerman uses the example of Victorian London to suggest that economic growth is sustainable and that a market-based approach is best. He notes that the growth of traffic in the nineteenth century, when horses where used for hackney cabs, the taxis of the day, should have led to the city being buried under horse dung.[6] Nevertheless, disaster was averted by the introduction of the combustion engine, which banished the horse from London's streets. Thus, environmental problems are best left to the market, and conscious intervention may be inappropriate.

There are other ways of narrating environmental history. Although I would argue that there is good evidence of effective communal management of resources and a clear record of commons being destroyed with resulting environmental injustice, I am also aware that any narrative risks biasing the story that is being told. A neutral view that is untainted by narrative is likely to be impossible, as is argued by historians such as Hayden White.[7] In concluding, I want to make suggestions for a more sustainable future but also to provide some healthy doubt. The environmental history of the commons throws up useful questions that we must ask ourselves if future generations are to enjoy a comfortable future. We need to discuss how environmental historians can continue to research the commons so we can learn more. We need to ask why many environmental policies appear to be failing at present and to what extent commons-based solutions provide an alternative. The question of a wider economy of social sharing, which provides an alternative to extractivist capitalism, is also a vital area of debate. Equally, questions of how the threats to commons are countered and whether new commons can be sustained demand considerable thought. As the novelist Thomas Pynchon notes, "If they can get you asking the wrong questions, they don't have to worry about the answers."[8] Asking the right or at least better questions is important.

How Do We Research the Commons?

The more we learn about environmental history, the better we should be able to create an environmentally sustainable future. The environmental history of the commons is a relatively new area of study, but as this book has outlined, it is a vital one. A misreading of the historical record can have devastating results. The notion of the "tragedy of the commons" has some value, but the open unmanaged commons can be abused, and Garrett Hardin's paper fails to examine actual commons. As has been clearly established, many were well managed, and where they were unmanaged, human populations and their productivity were low enough to prevent overexploitation. Yet arguments similar to those of Garrett Hardin have been used to justify enclosure over centuries, accompanied by loss of liberty for commoners, reduction in biodiversity, and environmental degradation.

Understanding the historical commons involves undertaking research. This simple fact is at the heart of Elinor Ostrom's work. She has argued that economists, in particular, create models that may have some validity but need to be tested and refined by looking at real-life examples. This may seem obvious but still may need to be spelled out. In turn, practical research is influenced by theory. Different theoretical frameworks encourage us to ask different questions and perhaps to come to different conclusions.

There are numerous schools of thought in historiography. A useful way to borrow from commons researchers to improve the quality of research into the commons is to embrace the notion of pluralism. Legal theorists of indigenous commons have coined the term *legal pluralism*, which is the notion that rather than there being a single legal system, different legal systems may overlap. In countries that have seen European occupation, like Australia and Canada, formal law typically exists alongside customary indigenous law. Legal pluralists argue that both need to be acknowledged. In a British context, Christopher Rodgers and his colleagues use a legal pluralist approach to investigate the environmental history of the English commons. They argue that customary informal law shaped the commons as well-codified official law. Both Elinor and Vincent Ostrom investigated how overlapping institutions that look messy to outsiders may provide more democratic and efficient governance than central unified control. The Ostroms believed that a polycentric or pluralist approach to both practical management of resources and theory is often appropriate.

I would agree that we need a similar messy overlapping set of theoretical perspectives to research the commons. This book has outlined at various points a diverse set of approaches to commons research across disciplines, including geography, law, history, and economics. Three broad approaches can be identified in examining the history of commons—that of Elinor Ostrom, that of Karl Marx, and the culturally specific approach of many anthropologists. Rather than seeking to identify one single true approach, it may be more valuable to note that all three provide useful insights. For example, a dimension of power and conflict needs to be examined along with questions of functional management by commoners. Thus, both Marx and Elinor Ostrom provide essential, contrasting, and complementary perspectives. A number of scholars combine these two perspectives to some extent, showing the ways that commons worked in an historical context and the devastation of much commons by colonial invasion. The central role that is played by culture in the evolution and destruction of commons, with cultural assumptions either supporting commons or justifying their destruction, is another perspective to which researchers need to be sensitive. Although far from reductionist, both the Marx and Ostrom approaches may downplay cultural factors, so the rich cultural perspectives developed by anthropologists, who in turn are intellectually diverse, need to be acknowledged as well. Commons have meanings for commoners that are not always well described by economic motivation alone, and economics itself is often part of wider cultural and social systems. Indigenous people in Australia who sing to the land or Mongolian herders who believe that dragons own the soil provide beautiful examples of commoning beyond cost-benefit analysis and class struggle.

Theoretical frameworks, however sophisticated, can act as metaphor: the framework encourages researchers to examine particular aspects of a question and to disregard others, which leads to a danger of reification. Reification occurs when a theoretical concept is mistaken for an actual object during the process of research. Economics is apparently particularly prone to reification, but it is a potential problem in any academic field. Commons can be reified. For example, property rights can be informal and subtle, but there is a danger that researchers will understand them in overformalized and crude ways. There is a risk of squeezing real-life examples into the conceptual categories that we use. We cannot do without conceptual categories, but we must be aware of the danger of possible distortion in using them. Theory must be nuanced and, as I have argued, plural. Most significantly, theory should be made explicit. Without making theory explicit, the researcher is more likely to fall back on commonsense notions that may be false or at best oversimplified.

The practical task of researching historical commons can also be challenging. Customary law may not give rise to documentary evidence, and indigenous societies may have oral but no written records. However, as Elinor Ostrom shows, the need to manage commons carefully can give rise to rich archival material. Records of stints, rulings over disputes, and log books used by commons "tallymen" or women or reeves may all be available. As noted in chapter 1, the case studies that Elinor

Ostrom describes had detailed and long recorded histories that gave rise to thick archives. The amount of material available for those who seek to study English commons is remarkable. As E. P. Thompson notes, the material is so rich that it may prove challenging to work with: "A novice in agricultural history caught loitering in those areas with intent would quickly be despatched."[9] Robert Netting, in his study of Törbel, was able to use family commons records that stretched back three hundred years. Overload may be a problem, too, where records are extensive. Netting labored for many years on his investigation of one Swiss commons.[10]

The assumptions of those who produce historical records also shape the history that is told. This can be a particular problem in researching commons. In some circumstances, the voices of the commoners may be absent from the historical record or only faintly heard. The records may be written by enclosers, and the former commoners may be silenced. The assumptions of those observing the commons can distort the record strongly, so records, especially those beyond the technical data logged by commoners, need to be treated with a critical understanding. For example, the First Nation historian Christopher Hannibal-Paci notes that historical documents produced by explorers and traders who visited the communities of the Cree and Ojibwe must be treated with care. He argues that anyone reading these documents should use a number of filters to understand their context, including what they left out and what they emphasized:

Most traders, explorers and missionaries had in mind the possibilities of establishing trade (precious metals and goods, i.e. beaver) and transportation routes (western passage and Mandans). Often rare and unique objects-occurrences were recorded and the mundane, for example what was served for dinner and who cooked, was left out. Tropes such as the dying noble savage and motives such as the harvesting of souls often coloured how Cree and Ojibwe were represented to the old and new world.[11]

Along with careful treatment of historical records, ecology needs to be carefully integrated into studies of the commons. Ecological assumptions may be made without recourse to adequate research evidence. Techniques used by environmental archeologists (such as pollen analysis and soil profiling) should, wherever possible, be used to provide more grounded evidence of actual environmental conditions. Environmental and social change must also be assumed: commons have been in flux, and the idea of stable ecological equilibrium is increasingly rejected by ecologists. Such ecological data should be linked with a study of social history. William Cronon's work on New England provides an excellent example of such an approach.[12] The case studies discussed by Elinor Ostrom and by E. P. Thompson in *Customs in Common* also link ecological and social history perspectives. Most recently, Christopher Rodgers and his colleagues have produced a superb environmental history covering detailed case-study examples of four commons in England and Wales. They argue that more international comparative research is needed to help us understand how commons work. We should also ask how commoners might be resourced to write their own histories and learn from the experience of others. The Digital Library of the Commons, available at http:// dlc.dlib.indiana.edu/dlc, provides a useful open-source research resource that we can contribute to and share.

Archaeological techniques also should be used as commons give rise to physical traces that can be examined. In 2002, the historical conservation body English Heritage undertook a survey of England's town commons. Towns had commons that were used to provide grazing, other usufruct rights, and space for public events such as fairs. Over fifty surviving town commons were surveyed, and some were examined in great detail to record changes in their use over time. English Heritage integrated its archeological findings with the work of commons historians such as E. P. Thompson.[13]

How Can the Commons Sustain the Environment?

There are number of grounds for arguing that commons can help to create a sustainable future. The prevailing assumption has been that either strong state regulation (such as antipollution laws) or the use of market mechanisms (such as carbon trading) can be used to solve environmental problems. Regulation has often succeeded. For example, air pollution legislation introduced during the 1950s in the United Kingdom transformed London from a smog zone where thousands died of pollution-related diseases to a far cleaner city. From blue whales to Southern African lions, species have been protected by legislation.

But legislation may be inflexible and lead to unintended consequences. Usually, the alternative is seen to be some form of market-based environmentalism, where taxes and charges are used to make environmental damage more expensive. Appropriate action is encouraged by subtle changes to prices, and if environmentally appropriate choices are cheaper and polluting more expensive, then self-interest can be used to promote sustainability. Unfortunately, market mechanisms such as carbon taxes and forms of emissions trading may price out the poorest and have a relatively small effect on environmental problems. Despite global summits to try to stabilize climate, levels of carbon dioxide and other greenhouse gases have continued to rise. The use of carbon trading has so far failed to reduce emissions and has a number of negative consequences. Elinor Ostrom cites Larry Lohmann, an activist from Carbon Trade Watch, who argues that such artificial markets are often flawed.[14] She notes that "Scientists criticize the carbon accounting methodology as a 'one size fits all' policy that does not account for the diversity of ecosystems involved and may penalize actions that help restore forest ecosystems rather than destroy them."[15]

The current crisis of global economics since the financial collapse of 2008 and the stalling of efforts to deal with climate change via market mechanisms are just two reasons that commons are likely to become more significant. There is much rhetoric about managing global commons from both radical voices like Bolivian president Evo Morales and more established figures and institutions, but is the creation of planetary commons possible or desirable?

The phrase *global commons* is often used by policymakers but seems distant from the local commons discussed in previous chapters in this book. Oceans and atmosphere are unowned and so can, it is assumed, suffer from the classic Garrett Hardin "tragedy of the commons." Global overfishing and climate change are examples here. The assumption is that global agreements can be constructed on a planetary scale to enclose commons and introduce management rules to prevent free riders from causing degradation. Such an approach can be combined with market mechanisms. For example, climate change has been tackled via market-based instruments that mean that carbon trading is used to achieve limits to emissions. Global agreements have had some value: the Montreal Treaty of 1988 led to the banning of chlorofluorocarbons (CFCs), and the damaged ozone layer may eventually heal.

A purely local approach to commons would seem deficient in tackling such global problems, and Elinor Ostrom accepts the need for international agreements. However, she notes that the use of polycentric institutions described by her and her husband, Vincent, may be of value in dealing with climate change. She did not believe that there was one single ideal solution that could be used to reduce greenhouse gas emissions and suggested instead that attempts to develop different strategies could promote useful experimentation.[16]

Ecology is a complex science, and it might be thought that ecological management would require centralized control

because centralized bodies can best gather the scientific knowledge needed to learn how ecosystems could be maintained.
Yet environments are often so local that distant policymakers
cannot manage them appropriately. The maintenance of local
commons over historical time deepens such knowledge, and as
Elinor Ostrom argues, local people are also motivated to maintain their local environments because their continued prosperity depends on managing them sustainably. The Barabaig from
the highlands around Mount Hanang in Tanzania typically
know that overgrazing could wreck the land around the rivers,
so they rotate their cattle:

As herds of livestock are brought to the river margins every day, whatever the season, they know that the forage there is needed by those
who are watering their stock. If others are allowed to graze perma-
nently, this forage would soon be depleted and not available to those
who go there to draw water. This would ultimately result in destruction of the land through over-grazing and damage from concentration
of hoof traffic. The Barabaig, therefore, have a customary rule that
bans settlement at the river margins and denies herders the right to
graze the forage if they are not there to water their stock.[17]

Global conservation of global commons requires the conservation of local commons. In recent decades, the Barabaig
have had their communal land stolen and their rights abused.
The Minority Rights Group notes that since 1969, it has been
in conflict with the Tanzania Canada Wheat Project, which has
taken over 400,000 hectares of the best grazing land. The Barabaig have endured serious repression in their battles over land,
including house burnings, confiscation of cattle, destruction of
rights of way, desecration of sacred sites (including graves by
plowing), and physical assault. In 1989, the government removed their customary land rights and prosecuted the Barabaig "for trespassing on land they considered their own."[18]

Elinor Ostrom has noted that commons are generally most
effective at a local level, where relatively small numbers of people can learn to work with each other, reducing the possibility

of a free-rider problem. As discussed in this book, this is broadly confirmed by the historic record of common-pool property management. However, some relatively large commons have been successful. Commons regimes, despite the possibility of conflict, often work with each other and can overlap. Intercommoning, where different communities share territory, has succeeded in managing resources in the past.

Commons also can be nested into larger units. The Internet, World Wide Web, and free and open-source software also suggest that new and larger commons can be created. Despite some problems and limitations, *Wikipedia* is a well-known example of a global multilingual commons where property rights are constructed and global participation is possible. Larger-scale commons might be managed with input from wikis. Where necessary, however, global management of commons has to be implemented, and as Elinor Ostrom observed, such implementation occurs at local, subnational, and national levels. Appropriate structures need to be in place at these levels. Yet the enclosure of commons on a planetary basis is flawed, and commons are unlikely to be meaningfully managed efficiently, ecologically, or democratically on this basis.

Purely central action will not lead to good policy for a whole series of reasons that are well illustrated by present climate management. Policymakers may lack appropriate knowledge of the situation on the ground, monitoring may not work, individuals and communities may lack motivation, and powerful interests may bend the policy process to serve their own interests. More fundamentally, the current demands of the global economy tend to place increasing pressure on the environment. Kenneth R. Olwig, professor of landscape history, has argued that instead of dealing with climate change by producing more renewable energy and continuing with economic growth that degrades the environment, we should focus on promoting "historically produced sustainable commons."[19]

In their book *Commonwealth*, Michael Hardt and Antonio Negri examine the global politics of commons and the threat of enclosure. They argue that the present capitalist economy acts as a kind of invisible force field operating "on all kinds of production."[20] The market economy tends to shape everything that it comes into contact with, like a gravitational field that has power but cannot be seen directly. The free-rider metaphor, which is used to justify global enclosure of commons, ignores the fact that market-based economics is a key source of environmental damage. The present global economy drives an extractivist approach that is based on taking and using resources to fuel economic growth. This has difficult implications for environmental sustainability. Therefore, constructing a commons economy is more important, perhaps, than simply attempting to reduce the side effects of an unsustainable economic model through global legislation. If we are to be good ancestors, we need to ask ourselves how to develop an economic system that protects our children and their children and so on rather than one that erodes their inheritance.

How Do We Socially Share?

A high-growth consumer society makes huge demands on the environment. However many ways that we find to manage land, seas, air, and forests in an environmentally sensitive way, increasing consumption tends to place increasing pressure on them. Yet commoning might, in a broader sense, allow us to consume more selectively and thereby reduce our environmental impact. Thus, the ecological virtues of common-pool property can be extended further. The notion of environmentally sustainable usufruct can be seen as central to the concept of common-pool property and perhaps to the very notion of sustainability. The concept of social sharing, developed by Yochai Benkler, extends the notion of common-pool property rights.

Commons is common—in land economics and in the virtual territory of the World Wide Web—but social sharing can extend commons to the use of physical goods. In his paper titled "'Sharing Nicely': On Shareable Goods and the Emergence of Sharing as a Modality of Economic Production,"Benkler gives examples of carpooling and computer use. He argues that social sharing can occur where goods have more capacity than an individual private owner needs. The SETI Institute's mission is a good example:

SETI@home is the paradigmatic Internet-based distributed computing project. It harnesses idle processor cycles of about 4,500,000 users around the world. The users download a small screen saver. When the users are not using their computers, the screen saver starts up, downloads problems for calculation—in the case of SETI@home, radio astronomy signals to be analyzed for regularities as part of the search for extraterrestrial intelligence—and calculates the problems it has downloaded. Once the program calculates a solution it automatically sends its results to the main site. The cycle continues for as long as, and every time that, the screen saver is activated, indicating that the computer is idle from its user's perspective. Using this approach, SETI@home became the fastest "supercomputer" in the world, capable of performing, as of the summer of 2003, calculations at a speed sixty percent faster than the NEC Earth Simulator, formally the fastest supercomputer in the world.[21]

The SETI project might seem a long way from environmental history and a sustainable future, yet the practice of social sharing could help us to reduce negative human effects on the environment by cutting consumption. By avoiding built-in obsolescence, social sharing means that resource use can be reduced as goods are made to last longer. In their book *What's Mine Is Yours: The Rise of Collaborative Consumption*, the British writers Rachel Botsman and Roo Rogers have promoted the idea of collaborative consumption. They argue that collaborative consumption means that we can share our way to sustainability, suggesting that rather than owning goods outright, we can hire or borrow them to reduce our effects on the environment.[22] Collaborative consumption advocates argue that there is a difference between quantitative economic growth (which may be unsustainable) and economic developmen (which may raise the quality of life with reduced physical effects on the environment).

Historical examples of social sharing might help us to imagine how a future sustainable society might work to reduce poverty without wrecking the biosphere. In his study of the community of Törbel in the Swiss Alps, Netting noted that each family owned its own farm implements, but larger "more costly devices like the huge cheesemaking kettles and wine presses were owned by cooperative associations of users, or, in the case of the bread bakery, by the community as a whole."[23]

Such examples might also further disengage us from Malthusian and cornucopian approaches that tend to disempower us by suggesting either that little can be done to tackle inevitable environmental degradation (Malthus) or that little or nothing need be done (cornucopia).

Green movements and environmentalists have criticized conventional forms of economic growth and development because they are unsustainable and also because they believe that they have an impoverishing effect quality of life. John Ruskin, the nineteenth-century art critic and social commentator, provides an example of this critique. Ruskin argued that much wealth was in fact "illeth" and rather than contribute to our well-being made us sick. In Ruskin's view, we should reject production that promotes illness rather than health. The creation of ugly products and weapons, for example, makes human beings weaker as it makes the economy stronger. He looked back to a distinction made by Aristotle between *oikonomia* (which was about the management of resources to promote all-round human development) and *chrematistics* (which was about the accumulation of money).[24]

In a similar vein although for rather different purposes, Karl Marx, in his discussion of commodity, also drew on Aristotle to make a distinction between *use* and *exchange* values. Much modern economic activity is about accumulating exchange values rather than increasing human access to useful things. This distinction is perhaps valuable when we think about commons. The Heinrich Böll Foundation, a think tank named after the late German novelist and closely associated with the German Green Party, produced a report titled *The Commons: Prosperity by Sharing* that notes that commons includes air, water, land, knowledge, and software. Commonly owned resources allow us to live from day to day and underpin our economy, so threats to the commons from enclosure present a serious problem. Commons need to be nurtured and defended from erosion.[25] The foundation argues that green politics and economics must embrace the notion of the commons:

An epoch in modern history has ended. The growth imperative of market capitalism is evidently endangering the ecosystem. Confidence in governments as reliable steward of people's interests has been shaken. Therefore, a new path forward is coming into focus: The commons! The commons is about reclaiming, sharing and self-governing resources that belong to everyone. As a form of governance it is defending traditional or building new social and institutional systems for managing our resources—water and land, knowledge and seeds, genes and the atmosphere—based on the principles of equity and sustainability. The commons is a practical means for re-inventing society in ways that markets and governments are unable or unwilling to entertain. Commons does not mean resources alone are centre stage; of higher importance are the relationships among us, the commoners, our ways of commoning![26]

From natural resources to the human conceptual commons of language, many areas of life are held in common without private ownership. These provide the basis for wider activity. As Aristotle might have said (despite his skepticism about commons), even chrematistics cannot exist without commons.

Social sharing can make a huge contribution by improving access to goods and services so that individuals can improve their prosperity if such prosperity is defined in terms of access to what is useful. The commons in land, as we have seen, has allowed human beings to live more easily. Commoners have gathered food, firewood, medicinal herbs, and fuel to sustain their communities for thousands of years.

The information commons, exemplified by *Wikipedia*, means that individuals can enjoy all manner of culture and information on the World Wide Web, which would have been enclosed before the creation of these new commons. A new socioeconomic system is emerging and is based on such new commons. The Internet allows large groups of people who may live thousands of miles away from each other to cooperate in producing goods and services. According to Yochai Benkler, Lawrence Lessig, and other legal theorists, this system of peer-to-peer production is a system of production based on cooperative creativity rather than the price mechanism of the free market or top-down hierarchies that are associated with central planning and corporate control.

We can reduce negative environmental effects by using sharing to reduce our consumption. Collaborative consumption has an important role in reducing the need for resources. Benkler has argued that whenever an individual user requires only a small percentage of the capacity of a good, service, or resource, the potential for social sharing exists. Within a conventional market-based economy, collaborative consumption is becoming more widespread, which reduces resource throughput. Can we talk of a commons in automobiles and bicycles? Systems of market-based rentals, voluntary forms of sharing such as carpooling, and library services for a range of physical goods point toward an economy where the accumulation of cash shrinks and access to all that is useful increases.

The instrumental need to gain money is the motivation for many careers. Intrinsic motivation—production for the love of production—is another potential virtue of commons-based production. The creativity of peer-to-peer processes is also important and a source of economic development of humanity in a wider sense. The peer-to-peer approach, where software is placed on the Net and individuals are encouraged to collaborate to produce better versions, has already led to an explosion in creativity.

An economy based on increasing levels of social sharing does not preclude private ownership but has a number of benefits compared to an economy where such individual ownership is the main or only way of consuming. It reduces resource use, promotes collaboration, enhances creativity, and reduces material want. How we create a commons of land, other environmental resources, and even physical goods opens up a set of new questions that demand debate. A commons-based system of manufacture creates many challenges. However, as chapter 3 on the politics of commons indicates, the key issue may not be the functionality of commons but the need to overcome political resistance to common-pool property arrangements. As good ancestors, we should resist the erosion of commons. This understanding means that we need to return to a discussion of questions of power, politics, and above all, strategy.

How Do We Fight the Crab?

Formerly, when animals were people, a giant crab, called Ugkaju, commanded an army composed of ants and fish that killed the strongest warriors, . . . Ugkaju struck the water with its clamp forming floods that drowned the people. The warriors could not defeat it. Finally, the weakest animal met to plan an attack. They were the armadillos and some small birds that make their nests in earth holes. According to the plan, they were digging tunnels that arrived at the house of Ugkaju. The next time that the giant crab struck the water, the little animals opened the tunnels and all the water ran by them and he was in dry. Then the paucar took its lance and killed him.[27]

The story of Ugkaju is used by the Awajun, a Peruvian indigenous group from the Amazon, to illustrate their fight for the commons. Although much has been written about the viability of the commons, the elephant (or the giant crab) in the room is the often violent destruction of the commons. The Awajun defeated Inca and Spanish attempts to take their territory. Using nonviolent direct action, legal challenges, and the World Wide Web, they are currently fighting the incursions of multinational companies and the central government of Peru. Indigenous people across the world continue to resist attempts to destroy their commons.

Time after time, commons have been enclosed with the threat of violence, and commoners have been displaced. A key set of questions that need to be asked about a sustainable future is how to defend, deepen, and extend the commons in the face of violent attacks.

Much work on commons assumes that commons are shaped largely by local factors and discusses the functionalism of commons, but the history of commons is also a history of assault and defense. The debates over functionalism are relevant but are only a part of the study of commons. The "tragedy of the commons" theme has been used to justify enclosure, while Elinor Ostrom's work has been used to defend the commons. Political and strategic approaches to the commons can be found in the work of Karl Marx, philosophers such as Gilles Deleuze and Félix Guattari, as well the autonomist Marxist authors Michael Hardt and Antonio Negri. Latin American left governments, indigenous organizations, commons-oriented think tanks, and nongovernmental organizations such as On the Commons have, in varied ways, sought to campaign for commons.

Marx argued that capitalism eroded the commons, yet, in his opinion, by promoting economic accumulation, capitalism raises the productive forces through industrialization and helps to create a new political agent, the working class, that can restore democratically owned common property as the basis of a new society. Marx's son-in-law, Paul Lafargue, summarized such a view, arguing that in the ancient past, property such as land or cattle was common to all members of a "clan" and that "Communism was the cradle of humanity." Lafargue argued that "the work of civilisation is twofold: while on the one hand it destroys, on the other hand it reconstructs; while it broke into pieces the communist mold of primitive humanity, it was building up the elements of a higher and more complex form of communism."[28]

There is some evidence that Marx himself rejected such a linear view of history, however. For example, he explored the idea that in Russia the peasant Mir, a communal system of land ownership and farming, would allow for the recreation of commons without the need to move through and beyond a capitalist economy.[29] Marx's broad framework has been at best delayed or at worst destroyed. The international working class has not yet re-created the commons. Marxists have generally replaced Marx's belief in the commons with forms of state-based central planning, and Marx's interest in the commons seems to have been largely forgotten by communists. Workers, however, have tried to create commons. In Britain during the 1970s, the workers at Lucas Aerospace constructed an alternative production plan.[30] This involved developing alternatives to the military equipment that was being built at Lucas Aerospace, with the workers showing how they could produce road-rail buses, equipment for children with disabilities, and a range of other socially useful products. The plan was not put into practice, but it illustrates a communal, self-managed alternative that is in line with Marx's thinking. Peer-to-peer production of manufactured goods is possible, and workers' control is necessary for the commons.

The often rather impenetrable works of French philosophers Gilles Deleuze and Félix Guattari, dripping in obscure
terminology and in debt to the challenging work of the psy-
chologist Jacques Lacan and European philosophers such as
Friedrich Nietzsche and Baruch Spinoza, have described a
process of deterritorialization. Deterritorialization, they argue,
occurs where a political territory is invaded and its rules and
norms are destroyed and replaced by new rules and norms in
a process of reterritorialization. Property rights can be seen as
the codes or DNA of society. Deterritorialization involves removing them and replacing them via reterritorialization with
new rules or to be more precise, removing codes from their
context and rearticulating them. The process of primitive accumulation, identified by Marx, where commons are enclosed
to make way for capitalist expansion, can be linked to these
concepts. The destruction of the European commons and the
commons of empires like those of the Inca and Aztec by the
Spanish can be understood in terms of de- and recoding. The
coding point is illuminating, with Deleuze and Guattari illus-
trating this understanding poetically with the suggestion that a
club is a deterritorialized branch.[31] What was once a living part
of a tree is ripped out of its context and placed in a new context. The branch is deterritorialized: it no longer acts as part of
a tree that gives life to leaves that absorb sunlight but instead
is recoded and acts as a human weapon. Jeanette Neeson in
her book on the enclosure of the English commons quotes the
novelist John Berger, who wrote "Do you know. . . what the
trees say when the axe comes into the forest? . . . When the axe
comes into the forest, the trees say: 'Look! The handle is one
of us!'"[32] Property rights give power to human beings to access
and use resources, and as such, they are intrinsic to questions
of political power. Property rights provide the means to code
and recode. The current battles to enclose the World Wide Web
by companies, attempts to extend copyright, and legislation to

establish access to countryside for citizens are conflicts that involve property right coding.

Michael Hardt and Antonio Negri, in a rereading of Marx that is strongly influenced by the philosopher Baruch Spinoza as well Deleuze and Guattari, see information commons as key. Hardt and Negri stress immaterial labor and the actions of "the multitude" rather than the working class or indigenous as creators of potential commons.[33] They argue that intellectual and emotional work increasingly produce value in the twenty-first century. Commons, especially in cyberspace, are increasingly central to the production of such value and social subjectivity. The individuals who create such value are the multitude. Although this might sound obscure, the explosion of social media activity and the financial strength of Google, Amazon, and Facebook are excellent illustrations of the way that we all increasingly produce value in a new information economy.

More concretely, perhaps, Latin American leftist governments have taken elected power and have promoted, via the notion of twenty-first-century socialism, the idea of grassroots ecological collective production. They have been influenced in their wider policymaking by notions of socialism as decentralist democratic provision of goods rather than the central planning of the former Soviet Union. René Ramirez, the influential Ecuadorian planning minister, noted that "The perspective of Elinor Ostrom goes in hand in hand with the idea of good living. What she says is something fundamental, that collective interaction can handle the [management of] natural resources more efficiently."[34]

The notion of *buen vivir*, the indigenous concept of "good living" (that is, sustainable living) has been promoted globally by Bolivia's president, Evo Morales, other indigenous thinkers and politicians, and grassroots social movements. These developments are welcome, but they are also problematic. Conflicts over environmental issues continue in countries like Bolivia,

Ecuador, and Venezuela, all of which remain strongly dependent on extracting fossil fuels including oil and gas, despite such rhetoric of "good living."

Outside of cyberspace, the radical left, and some indigenous people, commons movements have grown more slowly, but organizations such as On the Commons in the United States and the Heinrich Böll Foundation in Germany are increasingly active. On the Commons seeks to educate citizens and policymakers. It is strongly opposed to the privatization of resources and builds on the work of Elinor Ostrom, ecofeminists like the Indian writer Vandana Shiva, and indigenous leaders. It also promotes individual actions to conserve and create commons. On the Commons quotes the green economist and author of *Small Is Beautiful* Ernest Schumacher ("Perhaps we cannot raise the wind. But each of us can put up the sail, so that when the wind comes we can catch it"), and they list "fifty-one easy ways to promote a commons revolution," beginning with "Challenge the prevailing myth that all problems have private, individualized solutions" and continuing onward:

49. Think yourself as a commoner and share your enthusiasm. Raise the subject in conversation, art, professional circles, and organizations with which you are involved.

50. Launch a commons discussion group or bookclub with your neighbors and colleagues, or at your church, synagogue or temple.

51. Spread some hope around. Explain how commons-based solutions can remedy today's pressing problems.[35]

On the Commons also notes the importance of legal and political change as a way of promoting communing. For example, it opposes the extension of patents and copyrights that make it difficult to share ideas or culture for many decades.

The recent economic crises in Europe and the United States have challenged conventional market-based economics and notions of private property. Protest movements are increasingly advocates of commons. Political power at a national level is necessary to defend, extend, and deepen the commons. Governments guarantee property rights, and property rights are the basis of commons or their destruction. Pro-commons governments have a role to play, but although we might fault Ostrom's absence of discussion of the conflicted nature of commons under capitalism and imperialism, she provides an important caution to statist notions of a nonstate society. A government cannot proclaim commons from the top down. If commons are to have a real existence, they need be built on the ground by citizens who cooperate and learn. The new Forest Rights Act in India is a good example. After hundreds of years of attacking commons, both under British rule and after independence, the Indian government now recognizes them. But this new law has not entirely halted the erosion of the commons, as Elinor Ostrom has noted: "I would not agree if I am told that FRA is the panacea for all the problems related to people adversely affected by developmental projects. It is a good and powerful first step but not the solution."[36]

Nonetheless, the introduction of legislation that supports commons is important. In Latin America and to a lesser extent India, vigorous social movements based on peasant farmers and indigenous have had a positive political impact, which has helped stimulate political change and thereby promoted common-pool property.

Globally, the information commons has led to a culture of hacktivism that has been used to attack concentrations of power. The UK-based political scientist and commons activist Aaron Peters has noted that "the communicative ecology of the Internet"promotes economic activity through "'mass collaboration' and the rejection of traditional notions of intellectual property rights." He notes that this peer-to-peer economic approach is behind diverse projects including *Wikipedia*, Pirate Bay, hacktivism, Indymedia, the music of Tecnobrega and Girl Talk, as well as Cory Doctorow's writings.[37] He also argues that protest movements such as Occupy and the Arab Spring mobilizations have been infused with this spirit of commons and collective creativity.

The fight for commons in software and cyberspace has been linked to political activism, but libertarian Eric S. Raymond has taken a different approach, arguing that the best way to promote commons is by emphasizing its practical benefits.[38] His concept of open-source (as oppose to free) software has been growing rapidly in scope. It is also worth noting that one of the most successful contemporary examples of commoning, *Wikipedia*, was launched by another libertarian, Jimmy Wales. Wales, however, acknowledges the need to fight corporate-inspired forms of recoding such as legislation like the Stop Online Piracy Act (SOPA) that seeks to enclose the commons. The politics of commoning remains an essential but essentially contested area of discussion.

How Do We Love the Land?

Political change is necessary but far from sufficient to restore thriving commons. Commons can be destroyed from above and may be defended by political action, but they cannot be built from above. Venezuela is a good example of this. Communal councils are advocated at a state level but have to be constructed locally, which is impossible without grassroots enthusiasm.[39] Rules to provide communal property rights do not, on their own, allow the creation of effective collective management. Much of the 500,000 hectares of commons that still exist in England and Wales, particularly in the lowlands, is used mainly for recreational rather than agriculture activities. Practices such as the pollarding and coppicing of trees have been largely abandoned. Fires have damaged much heathland commons. Although climate change, arson, and accident may have played their part in this, plant waste from species such as bracken that used to be gathered by commoners today instead builds up, causing the risk of fire. Traditional forms of commons management have been lost across much of the United Kingdom and Western Europe and will be difficult to recreate.

In such contexts, the restoration of commons demands the creation of new traditions, which is not an easy task, and different forms of commoning lead to different environments. There is no one nature: human intervention creates different habitats with different implications for varied species, depending on the practices used. This understanding takes us back to problematic ideas of untainted wilderness. At its best, commoning may make sustainable use of resources, but it does not lead to a "pure" state of nature. Even in the absence of human interaction, the environment changes, and different forms of land management may give rise to different sustainable landscapes. If we are to be good ancestors, we need to ask how to construct alternative environments. Put simply, different management practices can mean that the same area of land can be maintained as grassland or made to become forest. Different crops, our animals, and different practices will lead to different environmental conditions. Thus, we need to create cultures of commoning, but we also need to ask which environments are the most appropriate products of commoning. Different forms of commoning give rise to different sustainable environments. For example, before 1904, the chestnut commons of Virginia were a creation of human action. They may have been created partly by the practice of burning learned from the Cherokees. Hogs that roamed the commons grubbed up other trees and bushes, helping the chestnuts. Without commoners, whether indigenous or not, the chestnuts might have been less dominant.[40] In England and Wales, many existing commons are heathland, but without management (particularly with grazing animals), they would become woodland. The environmental merits of heathland versus woodland are often aggressively debated, but both may be seen as environmentally sustainable.[41] Commoning that involved woodland clearance created such heathland in the past.

The question of how we love the land can be debated in other ways. Commons, as has been shown, are based on usufruct rights. This means access is allowed to selected individuals and communities on the condition that they maintain resources ecologically. Unlike purely private or state property, common-pool systems have sustainability built into them. But sustainability does not abolish environmental ethics. This point is nicely illustrated by the novelist Jules Verne's description of the eider duck hunters of Iceland:

In the early days of summer, the female of the eider, a pretty sort of duck, builds its nest amid the rocks of the fjords—the name given to all narrow gulfs in Scandinavian countries—with which every part of the island is indented. No sooner has the eider duck made her nest than she lines the inside of it with the softest down from her breast. Then comes the hunter or trader, taking away the nest, the poor bereaved female begins her task over again, and this continues as long as any eider down is to be found. When she can find no more the male bird sets to work to see what he can do. As, however, his down is not so soft, and has therefore no commercial value, the hunter does not take the trouble to rob him of his nest lining.[42]

The exploitation of the ducks is sustainable but is rather unethical, especially if viewed from the perspective of the bird.

One of the best-known examples of environmentally sustainable commons is the Maine lobster fisheries. Although the practice of lobster fishing might be seen as intrinsically unethical, local people have developed a commons that protects the lobsters from extinction. This is beneficial for the human part of the ecosystem because such careful maintenance means that the fishers can sustain their economy into the future. The system is no utopia, but its conservation record is better than that of state-regulated fisheries that have collapsed without the local collaborative element. It is not so good for the lobsters, perhaps: they are saved from extinction as a species locally but sacrifice members of their community to be boiled alive in the cooking pot. This book does not discuss the wider environmental ethics of sustainable use, but it is a rich and necessary part of being good ancestors. Commons potentially allow us to sustain exploitation of the nonhuman environment into the future, which is beneficial to future generations of humanity but still involves instrumental exploitation of other species. There are more questions to be answered in terms of ethical use. Communal management may be beneficial for humanity and the rest of nature, but it does not save the lobsters from a painful death. Although concern for the environment is necessary to move from an extractivist economy, it opens up further challenging questions because of the diverse potential of human interactions with the rest of nature.

Before Time People

The economic alternatives that most often are presented to us—either a growing capitalist economy or a centrally planned socialism—look entirely unsustainable. Approaches to planetary ecological problems, such as climate change, work within the context of a market-based economy. This economy is, at present, unrelentingly extractivist. Minerals, metals, fossil fuels, and other natural resources are transformed into commodities for sale, consumed, and thrown away, and the process begins again. The rapid economic growth of countries like India and China is leading to pressure to log and mine diverse habitats across the planet. From carbon trading to development of sources of renewable energy, the emphasis has been on finding ways to reduce negative environmental effects while sustaining increasing economic activity, but there are clear signs that this approach is failing. Despite a global framework with numerous conferences to tackle rising carbon dioxide emissions and other climate-change gases, emissions continue to rise. From the use of biofuels to the ineffectiveness of carbon trading, it is easy to criticize this approach, which by stressing the need for rising production fails to protect the basis of our collective prosperity.

The introduction of a centrally planned economy might appear to be a way of controlling production to promote conservation, and regulation has often reduced environmental problems. But the experiences of Soviet planning in Eastern Europe, China, and the former Soviet Union are discouraging. Although environmental quality was enshrined in the constitution of the USSR and Lenin took a break from other matters to establish natural parks in Russia, the overall sustainability record has been dire.[43] The draining of the Aral Sea, nuclear accidents, and severe pollution from acid rain are just some illustrations that this model has not provided a sustainable alternative to capitalism. It shares the capitalist system's emphasis on prioritizing industrial development, and additionally, via its centralization, it fails to take account of local environmental realities. Karl Marx endorsed the commons and showed an interest in ecology, but socialist and Marxist states have generally not provided good examples of environmental management. Cuba in recent decades has been an exception, and by introducing organic agriculture, strong wildlife protection, and renewable energy, it has provided a better example of ecologically sustainable socialism. Nevertheless, the gap between the green words of Marx and Engels and most examples of socialist practice suggests that anticapitalist alternatives to the market do not automatically protect the environment.

A Hayekian criticism of socialism is implicit in Ostrom's work. The economist Hayek argued that information is difficult to gather and that state-run economic planning is unlikely to work well because of the difficulties of dealing with dispersed knowledge. Shortages or surpluses of goods will be produced, we will have too many of some items and not enough of others, and chaos will result with long queues for the things we need. If, as Elinor Ostrom observed, socialism is statist, it is unlikely to be either economically efficient or environmentally benign. Hayek argues that markets help us deal with this knowledge problem, but capitalism pushes for unrestrained exploitation of the environment and increasingly can be criticized as centralized and insensitive to local needs.

The value of the commons concept in its varied manifestations is the possibility of creating an economic model that can, at least potentially, deliver both sustainability and prosperity. It can be argued that prosperity is possible only in the context of sustainability. In the commons, which is based on the principle of usufruct, resources can be exploited if it is possible to do so in a sustainable way. Commoners have a strong material interest in maintaining the commons because if they fail to do so, their survival is threatened. Planners in a distant office, whether in a hypothetical centrally planned economy or the headquarters of a global mining corporation or transnational supermarket, have a far weaker grasp of environmental conditions in the world outside their offices. If commons seem likely to slow economic accumulation of material goods, commons as social sharing provide a way of increasing access to resources while drastically reducing effects on the environment.

The arguments for systems of common-pool property rights as a basis for a sustainable future range from strong to overwhelming. To recap, communal property rights reduce resource use via social sharing. If more resources are shared instead of owned privately, it is possible to cut through the dilemmas of Malthusianism versus techno-optimism. Potentially less energy—fewer metals and minerals—would need to be dragged from the earth because more is shared, while access to material items is increased. This organizing principle is different from what is seen to be "natural" within market capitalism.

Communal property rights link the economic and the ecological. Ecological realities underpin the economic system, so
what is ecologically unsustainable becomes economically un-
desirable. Western European colonial empires maintained a
system of unsustainable plunder by colonizing new territories,
and such a tradition of extracting resources with little thought
for the future is apparent in our present global economy. This
is unsustainable. In contrast, the logic of commons is that
survival and prosperity require respect for ecological norms.
Although Elinor Ostrom did not criticize capitalism, she challenged the practice of what Mancur Olson termed "roving
band it" economies.[44] These use resources, devastate the local environment, and look for new lands and seas to plunder:
"large, high-powered boats can zoom into a local fishery, mas-
sively harvest it for a valuable species in the international market, and then move to another location before local authorities respond."[45] These roving bandits have depleted fisheries in
many parts of the world, according to Elinor Ostrom.

Commons provide a way of creating a more collective economic system without sacrificing flexibility and individual
choice. The growth of the new commons of information and
software illustrates how commons can be extended from the
purely local to the global. Growing a commons-based economic system is beyond the scope of this short book, but asking
how we do so provides another important set of questions that
we must ask ourselves if we are to be good ancestors.

When she was recognized by a politics association in 2008,
Elinor Ostrom noted the importance of asking how we develop
a sustainable society based on respect for the future:

Our problem is how to craft rules at multiple levels that enable humans to adapt, learn, and change over time so that we are sustaining the very valuable natural resources that we inherited so that we
may be able to pass them on. I am deeply indebted to the indigenous

peoples in the U.S. who had an image of seven generations being the appropriate time to think about the future. I think we should all reinstate in our mind the seven-generation rule. When we make really major decisions, we should ask not only what will it do for me today, but what will it do for my children, my children's children, and their children's children into the future.[46]

The "seven-generation rule" to which she refers is derived from the Haudenosaunee constitution. The term *Haudenosaunee* is translated as "They are building along house." This is the title preferred by its own citizens to describe the more commonly known Iroquois confederation made up of six nations of indigenous peoples—the Mohawk, Oneida, Onondaga, Cayuga, Seneca, and Tuscarora. Today they live in New York state, Quebec province, and Ontario province. The Haudenosaunee constitution, which has many interesting features (including systems of consensus decision making), stresses that future generations should be respected and that we should act as good ancestors.[47]

A major contribution to creating a sustainable future history will involve learning from indigenous people such as the Haudenosaunee. In fact, two of the towering figures who have sought to examine the historical record of the commons—Karl Marx and Elinor Ostrom—paid tribute to the Haudenosaunee. They both showed a passionate interest in Haudenosaunee political theory and the Haudenosaunee commons. Even today, after considerable erosion, indigenous societies remain varied and dynamic. Glenn Morris, a professor of political science in Denver and an indigenous leader, has argued that "communalism" is the norm for indigenous people. Although ideas of land held in common, respect for the environment, and consensus political decision making are usually seen in Western societies as radical, deviant, or at best desirable but unattainable, they are "neither new nor controversial in traditional indigenous societies."[48]

One lesson of environmental history, in general, and the study of commons, in particular, is that rather than excluding people to promote conservation, human management is vital. Instead of establishing nature parks and expelling indigenous and other peoples, sustainable management is possible. A notion of commons that includes both people and other species is beginning to replace the notion of "wilderness." In her book *The Blue Ridge Commons: Environmental Activism and Forest History in Western North Carolina*, environmental historian Kathryn Newfont argues that people can become energized to fight for the commons. She draws on William Cronon's analysis and argues for "a commons-inspired utilitarian model with a 'use but don't abuse' approach to public land management that valued multiple use and on-the-ground familiarity with the forest."[49]

Combatting climate change by keeping fossil fuels in the ground and by caring for carbon sinks such as forests means recognizing the rights of indigenous peoples and other users. A sustainable future might require a reindigenization of society in a twenty-first-century context. On a visit to Britain in 2010, the Peruvian indigenous leader Hugo Blanco explained to me that in his view indigenous identity ultimately is based not on ethnic categories but on cultures of communing and respect for nature within a context of social sharing. In this regard, rather than seeing indigenous people as part of history or even prehistory, we need to examine carefully their potential contributions to our collective future.

Indigenous people should not be romanticized. They have degraded their environments, and they have certainly changed them. William Cronon, for example, notes that indigenous love of huge fires in New England reduced tree cover and produced a parkland landscape in places.[50] Such intervention can increase biological diversity, but indigenous people may have hunted some species to extinction. Local indigenous knowledge or other forms of local knowledge can be inadequate, but indigenous people in many parts of the world have learned from mistakes in environmental management and developed new systems of ecological governance. A poetic illustration comes from Australia. The people of Erub in the Torres Straits talk of a group of "before time people" in this way. "Before time people" is a reference to ancestors who failed, in this case, to respect the commons, with the example of Maizab Kaur (Bramble Cay) showing the logic of a process of renewed environmental management. The "before time people" had to use magic to create Maizab Kaur because they had overexploited nesting seabirds and turtles and could no longer rely on them for food. Maizab Kaur was created some distance from where they lived to act as a kind of ecological larder, a protected reserve that could be monitored by elders. Those who abused the environment and did not respect Maizab Kaur were turned to stone. An understanding of the need to conserve the commons was made with reference to supernatural power and ancestral sacrifice: "Maura clan informants who today are middle-aged remember that as young hunters they would always inform an elder woman of the Maura clan of their intention to visit Maizab Kaur for turtles and seabird and turtle eggs; she would always say, 'why are you asking my permission? It belongs to you (as Meauram descendants)—' but they would nevertheless always ask."[51]

We need to ask how as "before time people" today, we can learn new rules and adapt old ones to sustain our future. The example of Maizab Kaur shows that past societies may have damaged the environment but also sometimes learned to find new ways of sustaining it. Realizing that we can ask questions and develop solutions that may work is more inspiring than an unrealistic view of past societies as prelapsian inhabitants of an ecological Eden or a pessimistic belief that humans automatically degrade their environment. So while championing the commons and calling for opposition to enclosure, I hope that this short book inspires further questions and some practical solutions. Asking appropriate questions is vitally important if we are to act as good ancestors who will be respected by our children and their children's children and so on and so on, as the Haudenosaunee and Ostrom like to say, for at least the next seven generations.

Notes

Foreword

1. Brian Donahue, *Reclaiming the Commons: Community Farms and Forests in a New England Town* (New Haven: Yale University Press, 1999), 51.

2. Stewart Brand, *The Media Lab: Inventing the Future at MIT* (New York: Viking Press, 1987), 202.

3. Nil Disco and Eda Kranakis, *Cosmopolitan Commons: Sharing Resources and Risks across Borders* (Cambridge, Mass.: MIT Press, 2013), 2.

4. Garrett Hardin, "The Tragedy of the Commons," *Science* 162 (December 13, 1968): 1243–1248, in *Managing the Commons*, ed. John Baden and Garrett Hardin (San Francisco: Freeman, 1977).

5. Although Hardin's theoretical interpretation of the commons was wholly abstract, Elinor Ostrom's work stresses real-world, historical examples.

6. Elinor Ostrom, *Governing the Commons: The Evolution of Institutions for Collective Action* (Cambridge: Cambridge University Press, 1990).

7. Wall, *Culture, Conflict, and Ecology*, 42.

1 Commons Ecology

1. E. P. Thompson, *Customs in Common* (Harmondsworth: Penguin, 1991), 126.

2. The Gypsies, "The Yetholm Gypsies," last modified 2004, accessed January 4, 2013, http://www.scottishgypsies.co.uk/yetholm.html.

3. Christopher Rodgers, Margherita Pieraccini, Eleanor A. Straughton, and Angus Winchester, *Contested Common Land: Environmental Governance Past and Present* (London: Earthscan, 2010), 28.

4. Timothy Morton, *Ecology without Nature: Rethinking Environmental Aesthetics* (Cambridge, Mass.: Harvard University Press, 2007), 162.

5. Jay Walljasper, "A New Way of Seeing the World: Protecting the Rights of Nature Depends on Understanding the Commons," *On the Commons*, last modified June 27, 2011, accessed January 4, 2013, http://www.onthecommons.org/magazine/new-way-seeing-world.

6. Massimo De Angelis and Stavros Stavrides, "On the Commons: A Public Interview with Massimo De Angelis and Stavros Stavrides," *E-flux* 17 (June 2010): 1.

7. Jeremy Waldron, *The Right to Private Property* (Oxford: Clarendon Press, 1988), 31.

8. H. Franz Schurmann, "Traditional Property Concepts in China," *Far Eastern Quarterly* 15(4) (1956): 507.

9. Elinor Ostrom, *Governing the Commons: The Evolution of Institutions for Collective Action* (Cambridge: Cambridge University Press, 1990), 30.

10. Rodgers et al., *Contested Common Land*, 1.

11. Yochai Benkler, *The Wealth of Networks: How Social Production Transforms Markets and Freedom* (London: Yale University Press, 2006), 60–61.

12. Ibid., 61.

13. William Hunter, *A Systematic and Historical Exposition of Roman Law in the Order of a Code* (London: Sweet & Maxwell, 1803), 399.

14. Karl Marx, *Capital*, vol. 3 (New York: International, 1976), 776.

15. Geoffrey Young, *The Country Eye: A Walker's Guide to Britain's Traditional Countryside* (London: George Philip, 1991), 90.

16. Rodgers et al., *Contested Common Land*, 36.

17. Stefan Brakensiek, "The Management of Common Land in North Western Germany," in *The Management of Common Land in North*

West Europe, c. 1500–1850, ed. Martina de Moor, Leigh Shaw-Taylor, and Paul Warde (Turnhout: Brepols, 2002), 225.

18. Carol M. Rose, "Romans, Roads, and Romantic Creators: Traditions of Public Property in the Information Age," *Law and Contemporary Problems* 66(1–2) (2003): 89–110.

19. Joel Kovel, *The Enemy of Nature: The End of Capitalism or the End of the World?* (London: Zed Books, 2007), 268.

20. Henry Maine, *Ancient Law* (London: Murray, 1876), 259.

21. William Cronon, *Changes in the Land: Indians, Colonists, and the Ecology of New England* (New York: Hill and Wang, 1983).

22. Minoti Chakravarty-Kaul, *Common Lands and Customary Law: Institutional Change in North India over the Past Two Centuries* (Delhi: Oxford University Press, 1996).

23. Martina de Moor, Leigh Shaw-Taylor, and Paul Warde, eds., *The Management of Common Land in North West Europe, c. 1500–1850* (Turnhout, Belgium: Brepols, 2002).

24. Maria Fernandez-Gimenez, "Land Use and Land Tenure in Mongolia: A Brief History and Current Issues," in *Rangelands of Central Asia: Proceedings of the Conference on Transformations, Issues, and Future Challenges*, ed. Donald Bedunah, E. Durant McArthur, and Maria Fernandez-Gimenez (Fort Collins, Colo.: U.S. Department of Agriculture, Forest Service, Rocky Mountain Research Station, 2006).

25. Dawn Chatty, "Environmentalism in the Syrian Badia: The Assumption of Degradation, Protection and Bedouin Misuse," in *Ethnographies of Conservation: Environmentalism and the Distribution of Privilege*, ed. David Anderson and Eeva Berglund (New York: Berghahn Books, 2003), 87–100.

26. Benkler, *The Wealth of Networks*.

27. Rodgers et al., *Contested Commons*.

28. Pranab Bardhan and Isha Ray, *Contested Commons: Conversations between Economists and Anthropologists* (Oxford: Blackwell, 2008).

29. Jimmy Wales, "Wales on *Wikipedia*," *Econtalk*, last modified 2009, accessed January 4, 2013, http://www.econtalk.org/archives/2009/03/wales_on_wikipe.html.

30. Peter Linebaugh, "Karl Marx, the Theft of Wood and Working Class Composition: A Contribution to the Current Debate," *Crime and Social Justice* 6 (1976): 5–16.

31. John Riddell, "From Marx to Morales: Indigneous Socialism and the Latin Americanization of Marxism," *Socialist Voice*, last modified June 19, 2008, accessed January 4, 2013, http://www.socialistvoice .ca/?p=299.

32. Friedrich Engels, *The Mark* (New York: New York Labor News Co., 1928).

33. Thompson, *Customs in Common*, 170.

34. Ibid., 105.

35. Ibid., 105–106.

36. Christopher Hill, *Winstanley: "The Law of Freedom" and Other Writings* (Cambridge: Cambridge University Press, 1973).

37. Peter Linebaugh, *The Magna Carta Manifesto: Liberties and Commons for All* (Berkeley: University of California Press, 2008).

38. De Angelis and Stavrides, "On the Commons: A Public Interview with Massimo De Angelis and Stavros Stavrides."

39. Michael Hardt and Antonio Negri, *Empire* (Cambridge, Mass.: Harvard University Press, 2000).

40. Michael Hardt and Antonio Negri, *Commonwealth* (Cambridge, Mass.: Harvard University Press, 2009).

41. George Caffentzis, "The Petroleum Commons," *Counterpunch*, last modified 2004, accessed January 4, 2013, http://www.counter punch.org/2004/12/15/the-petroleum-commons.

42. George Caffentzis, "A Tale of Two Conferences: Globalization, the Crisis of Neoliberalism and Question of the Commons, " paper prepared for the Alter-Globalization Conference, San Miguel de Al- lende, Mexico, August 9, 2004, p. 23, accessed January 4, 2013, http:// www.commoner.org.uk/?p=96.

43. Paul Burkett, *Marxism and Ecological Economics: Toward a Red and Green Political Economy* (Boston: Brill, 2006).

44. Kovel, *The Enemy of Nature*.

45. Garrett Hardin, "The Tragedy of the Commons," in *Managing the Commons*, ed. John Baden and Garrett Hardin (San Francisco: Freeman, 1977).

46. Alan Roberts, *The Self-Managing Environment* (London: Alison and Busby, 1979), 147.

47. Aristotle, *Politics* (Oxford: Clarendon Press, 1946), 1261b.

48. Hardin, "The Tragedy of the Commons," 20.

49. Ludwig Mises, *Human Action: A Treatise on Economics* (New York: Laissez Faire Books, 2008), 652.

50. Chatty, "Environmentalism in the Syrian Badia: The Assumption of Degradation, Protection and Bedouin Misuse."

51. Fred Pearce, *The Land Grabbers: The New Fight over Who Owns the Earth* (Boston: Beacon Press, 2013).

52. Elinor Ostrom, "A Long Polycentric Journey," *Annual Review of Political Science* 13 (2010): 1–23.

53. Ostrom, *Governing the Commons*, 1.

54. Mancur Olson, *The Logic of Collective Action: Public Goods and the Theory of Groups* (Cambridge, Mass.: Harvard University Press, 1965).

55. *The Economist*, "Elinor Ostrom," *The Economist*, June 30, 2012, last modified June 30, 2012, accessed January 4, 2013, http://www.economist.com/node/21557717.

56. Robert Wade, *Village Republics: Economic Conditions for Collective Action in South India* (Cambridge: Cambridge University Press, 1988).

57. Kate Ashbrook and Nicola Hodgson, *Finding Common Ground* (Henley-on-Thames: Open Spaces Society, 2010).

58. Chakravarty-Kaul, *Common Lands and Customary Law*.

59. Madhav Gadgil and Ramachandra Guha, *This Fissured Land: An Ecological History of India* (Oxford: Oxford University Press, 1997).

60. Susan Oosthuizen, "Archaeology, Common Rights and the Origins of Anglo-Saxon Identity," *Early Medieval Europe* 19(2) (2011): 153–181.

61. Ashbrook and Hodgson, *Finding Common Ground*, 5.

62. English Nature, no date, accessed January 4, 2013, http://www.english-nature.org.uk/citation/citation_photo/1002417.pdf.

63. R. A. Butlin, "Some Terms Used in Agrarian History: A Glossary," *Agricultural History Review* (1961): 98–104.

64. Donald McCloskey, "The Prudent Peasant: New Findings on Open Fields," *Journal of Economic History* 51(2) (1991): 343–355.

65. Ashbrook and Hodgson, *Finding Common Ground*, 6.

66. Rodgers et al., *Contested Common Land*, 41.

67. Bonnie McCay and Alyne Delaney, "Expanding the Boundaries of Commons Scholarship: The 2008 Conference of the International Association for the Study of the Commons," *International Journal of the Commons* 4(1) (2010): 213–225.

68. Fernandez-Gimenez, "Land Use and Land Tenure in Mongolia," 31.

69. David Sneath, *Changing Inner Mongolia: Pastoral Mongolian Society and the Chinese State* (Oxford: Oxford University Press, 2000).

70. Fernandez-Gimenez, "Land Use and Land Tenure in Mongolia," 33.

71. David Sneath, *The Headless State: Aristocratic Orders, Kinship Society, and Misrepresentations of Nomadic Inner Asia* (New York: Columbia University Press, 2007).

72. Sneath, *Changing Inner Mongolia*, 237.

73. Chakravarty-Kaul, *Common Lands and Customary Law.*

74. Thompson, *Customs in Common*, 170.

75. Ibid., 168.

76. Gadgill and Guha, *This Fissured Land: An Ecological History of India*, 134.

77. Ibid., 139.

78. Arundhati Roy, *Broken Republic Three Essays* (London: Hamish Hamilton, 2011).

79. Robert Netting, *Balancing on an Alp: Ecological Change and Continuity in a Swiss Mountain Community* (Cambridge: Cambridge University Press, 1981).

80. Ostrom, *Governing the Commons*, 62.

81. Netting, *Balancing on an Alp*, 61.

82. Ostrom, *Governing the Commons*, 63.

83. Margaret McKean, "Management of Traditional Common Lands (Iriaichi) in Japan," in National Research Council, *Proceedings of the Conference on Common Property Resource Management* (Washington, D.C.: National Academy Press, 1986), 559.

84. Ostrom, *Governing the Commons*, 73.

85. James Kho and Eunice Agsaoay-Saño, "Customary Water Laws and Practices in the Philippines," United Nations Food and Agriculture Organization, last modified 2005, accessed January 4, 2013, http://www.fao.org/fileadmin/templates/legal/docs/CaseStudy_Philippines.pdf.

86. Brakensiek, "The Management of Common Land in North Western Germany," 239.

87. Ostrom, *Governing the Commons*, 189.

88. William Beinart, "African History and Environmental History," *African Affairs* 99 (2000): 269–302.

89. Margaret McKean, "The Japanese Experience with Scarcity: Management of Traditional Common Lands," *Environmental Review* 6(2) (1982): 67.

90. Kirsten Ewers Andersen, "Communal Tenure and the Governance of Common Property Resources in Asia: Lessons from Experiences in Selected Countries," United Nations Food and Agriculture Organization, last modified 2011, accessed January 4, 2013, http://www.fao.org/docrep/014/am658e/am658e00.pdf.

91. Thompson, *Customs in Common*, 107.

92. James Loewen, *Lies across America: What Our Historic Sites Get Wrong* (New York: New Press, 1999), 414.

93. David Fischer, "Boston Common," in *American Places*, ed. William Leuchtenburg (New York: Oxford University Press, 2000), 128.

94. Nathan Sayre, "The Cattle Boom in Southern Arizona: Toward a Critical Political Ecology," *Journal of the Southwest* 41(2) (1999): 239–271.

95. Ian Simpson, Andrew J. Dugmore, Amanda Thomson, and Orri Vésteinsson, "Crossing the Thresholds: Human Ecology and Historical Patterns of Landscape Degradation," *Catena* 42(2) (2001): 175–192.

96. Rowland Ernle, *English Farming, Past and Present* (London: Longmans Green, 1912), 241.

97. Jeanette Neeson, *Commoners: Common Right, Enclosure and Social Change in England, 1700–1820* (Cambridge: Cambridge University Press, 1993).

98. Chakravarty-Kaul, *Common Lands and Customary Law*.

99. John Locke, *Two Treatises of Government* (London: Rivington, 1824), 145.

2   Culture in Common?

1. Christopher Rodgers, Margherita Pieraccini, Eleanor A. Straughton, and Angus Winchester, *Contested Common Land: Environmental Governance Past and Present* (London: Earthscan, 2010), 8.

2. Terry Eagleton, *The Idea of Culture* (Malden, Mass.: Blackwell, 2000), 1.

3. David Korten, *The Great Turning: From Empire to Earth Community* (San Francisco: Berrett-Koehler, 2006), 76.

4. James Acheson, *The Lobster Gangs of Maine* (Hanover, N.H.: University of New England Press, 1998), 65.

5. William Cronon, *Changes in the Land: Indians, Colonists, and the Ecology of New England* (New York: Hill and Wang, 1983).

6. Karl Marx, *Capital*, vol. 3 (New York: International Publishers, 1967), 776.

7. John Bellamy Foster, *Marx's Ecology: Materialism and Nature* (New York: Monthly Review Press, 2000).

8. Elinor Ostrom, "Engaging Impossibilities and Possibilities," in *Arguments for a Better World: Essays in Honor of Amartya Sen*, vol. 2, ed. Kaushik Basu and Ravi Kanbur (New York: Oxford University Press, 2008), 522.

9. Lionel Robbins, *An Essay on the Nature and Significance of Economic Science* (London: Macmillan, 1932), 16.

10. Erik Olin Wright, "Commentary 2: Sociologists and Economists on 'the Commons,'" in *Contested Commons: Conversations between Economists and Anthropologists*, ed. Pranab Bardhan and Isha Ray (Oxford: Blackwell, 2008), 238.

11. Jon Elster, *Nuts and Bolts for the Social Sciences* (Cambridge: Cambridge University Press, 1989), 13.

12. Wright, "Commentary 2: Sociologists and Economists on 'the Commons,'" 234.

13. Ben Fine, "Beyond the Tragedy of the Commons: A Discussion of *Governing the Commons: The Evolution of Institutions for Collective Action*," *Perspectives on Politics* 1(8) (2010): 583–586.

14. Peter Boettke and Paul Dragos Aligica, *Challenging Institutional Analysis and Development: The Bloomington School* (London: Routledge, 2009).

15. John R. Commons, *Legal Foundations of Capitalism* (Madison: University of Wisconsin Press, 1957).

16. Thráinn Eggertsson, "Economic Perspectives on Property Rights and the Economics of Institutions," Property Rights and the Performance of Natural Resource Systems, Workshop at the Beijer International Institute of Ecological Economics, 1993, p. 20, accessed January 4, 2013, http://dlc.dlib.indiana.edu/dlc/handle/10535/2330.

17. Elinor Ostrom, "Collective Action and the Evolution of Social Norms," *Journal of Economic Perspectives* 14 (3) (2000): 143.

18. Elinor Ostrom, Roy Gardner, and James Walker, *Rules, Games, and Common-Pool Resources* (Ann Arbor: University of Michigan Press, 1994).

19. Christopher Hannibal-Paci, "Lake Sturgeon: The Historical Geography of Lake Winnipeg Fishery Commons," paper presented at Crossing Boundaries, the Seventh Biennial Conference of the International Association for the Study of Common Property, Vancouver, British Columbia, Canada, June 10–14, 1998, accessed January 4, 2013, http://dlc.dlib.indiana.edu/dlc/handle/10535/2105.

20. Jean-Philippe Platteau, "Managing the Commons: The Role of Social Norms and Beliefs," in *Contested Commons: Conversations between Economists and Anthropologists,* ed. Pranab Bardhan and Isha Ray (Oxford: Blackwell, 2008), 28.

21. Margaret McKean, "Management of Traditional Common Lands (Iriaichi) in Japan," in National Research Council, *Proceedings of the Conference on Common Property Resource Management* (Washington, D.C.: National Academy Press, 1986).

22. Hartmut Zückert, "The Commons: A Historical Concept of Property Rights," in *The Wealth of the Commons*, ed. David Bollier and Silke Helfrich (Amherst, Mass.: Levellers Press, 2012).

23. Anil Gupta, "Building upon People's Ecological Knowledge: Framework for Studying Culturally Embedded CPR Institutions," paper presented at the Second Annual Conference of the International Association for the Study of Common Property, Winnipeg, Manitoba, September 26–29, 1991, accessed January 4, 2013, http://dlc.dlib.indiana.edu/dlc/handle/10535/588.

24. Fran Korten, "Elinor Ostrom Wins Nobel for Common(s) Sense," *Yes!* (February 2010).

25. Lawrence Krader, *The Ethnological Notebooks of Karl Marx: Studies of Morgan, Phear, Maine, Lubbock* (Assen: Van Gorcum, 1972), 335.

26. Lynn White Jr., "The Historical Roots of Our Ecologic Crisis," *Science* 155 (March 10, 1967): 1206.

27. Martin Yaffe, *Judaism and Environmental Ethics: A Reader* (Lanham, Md.: Lexington Books, 2001).

28. Seyyed Hossein Nasr, *Man and Nature: The Spiritual Crisis of Modern Man* (London: Unwin, 1976).

29. Daniel Dickinson, "Eco-Islam Hits Zanzibar Fishermen," BBC, last modified February 17, 2005, accessed January 4, 2013, http://www.bbc.co.uk/news/uk-england-berkshire-14677554.

30. John Hart, *Sacramental Commons: Christian Ecological Ethics* (Lanham, Md.: Rowman & Littlefield, 2006).

31. John Ikerd, "A New Jubilee of Agricultural Sustainability," paper presented at Rural Life Day 2003: Farming in the Sacramental Commons, a conference sponsored by the Social Concerns Office, Diocese of Jefferson City and MSR Center for Rural Ministry, Jefferson City, Missouri, December 6, 2003, 1.

32. Adam Smith, *The Wealth of Nations*, books 1–3 (Harmondsworth: Penguin, 1970), 119.

33. Karen Pittel and Dirk Rübbelke, "Characteristics of Terrorism," Economics Working Paper 09/103, CER-ETH-Center of Economic Research at ETH Zurich, 2009, 2.

34. Peter Beresford, *Ten Men Dead* (New York: Atlantic Monthly Press, 1987).

35. Marcel Mauss, *The Gift: Forms and Functions of Exchange in Archaic Societies* (New York: Norton, 1967).

36. Gareth Dale, *Karl Polanyi: The Limits of the Market* (Cambridge: Polity Press, 2010), 135.

37. William Cronon, *Changes in the Land: Indians, Colonists, and the Ecology of New England* (New York: Hill and Wang, 1983).

38. E. P. Thompson, *Customs in Common* (Harmondsworth: Penguin, 1991).

39. Marshall Sahlins, *Stone Age Economics* (London: Routledge and Kegan Paul, 1972), 1.

40. Ibid., 13.

41. Jeanette Neeson, *Commoners: Common Right, Enclosure and Social Change in England, 1700–1820* (Cambridge: Cambridge University Press, 1993), 41–42.

42. Ibid., 178.

43. Rodgers et al., *Contested Common Land*, 20.

44. K.D.M. Snell, *Annals of the Labouring Poor* (Cambridge: Cambridge University Press, 1985), 177.

45. Thompson, *Customs in Common*, 177.

46. Veronica Strang, *Uncommon Ground: Cultural Landscapes and Environmental Values* (Oxford: Berg, 1997), 225.

47. Ibid., 261.

48. E. P. Thompson, *Whigs and Hunters* (Harmondsworth: Penguin, 1975).

49. Pierre Bourdieu, *Distinction: A Social Critique of the Judgment of Taste* (Cambridge, Mass.: Harvard University Press, 1984).

50. Paul DeGeorges and Brian Reilly, "The Realities of Community Based Natural Resource Management and Biodiversity Conservation in Sub-Saharan Africa," *Sustainability* 1(3) (2009): 774.

51. Bruce Chatwin, *The Songlines* (London: Cape, 1987).

52. Rodgers et al., *Contested Common Land*, 25–26.

53. Thompson, *Customs in Common*, 103.

54. Michael Goldman, *Imperial Nature: The World Bank and Struggles for Social Justice in the Age of Globalization* (New Haven, Conn.: Yale University Press, 2005).

55. Adam Smith, *An Inquiry into the Nature and Causes of the Wealth of Nations* (London: Cooke and Hale, 1818), 167.

56. J. G. Farrell, *The Siege of Krishnapur* (London: Phoenix, 2011), 343.

3   Commons in Conflict

1. B. E. Fernow, *A Brief History of Forestry in Europe, the United States and Other Countries* (Toronto: University Press, 1907), 34.

2. David Roffe, "On Middan Gyrwan Fenne: Intercommoning around the Island of Crowland," *Fenland Research* 8 (1993): 80–86.

3. Ibid., 85.

4. E. P. Thompson, *The Making of the English Working Class* (London: Gollancz, 1963), 218.

5. Jeanette Neeson, *Commoners: Common Right, Enclosure and Social Change in England, 1700–1820* (Cambridge: Cambridge University Press, 1993).

6. Friedrich Engels, *The Mark* (New York: New York Labor News Co., 1928).

7. Karl Marx, *Capital: A Critique of Political Economy* (London: Penguin, 1976), 891–892.

8. Cliff Cobb, "A Brief History of Enclosure," *Progress* (January–February 2003): 15–17.

9. Joseph Clayton, *Robert Kett and the Norfolk Rising* (London: Martin Secker, 1912), 60.

10. James Stayer, *The German Peasant's War and Anabaptist Community of Goods* (Montreal: McGill-Queen's University Press, 1994), 107.

11. Simon Fairlie, "A Short History of Enclosure in Britain," *The Land* 1(7) (2009): 30.

12. Ibid.

13. William Cronon, *Changes in the Land: Indians, Colonists, and the Ecology of New England* (New York: Hill and Wang, 1983).

14. Alfred Cave, *The Pequot War* (Amherst: University of Massachusetts Press, 1996), 169.

15. Robert Coulter and Steven Tullberg, "Indian Land Rights," in *The Aggressions of Civilization: Federal Indian Policy since the 1880s*, ed. Sandra Cadwalader and Vine Deloria (Philadelphia: Temple University Press, 1984), 190–191.

16. William Cronon, "The Trouble with Wilderness; or, Getting Back to the Wrong Nature," in *Uncommon Ground: Rethinking the Human Place in Nature*, ed. William Cronon (New York: Norton, 1996).

17. Ralph H. Lutts, "Like Manna from God: The American Chestnut Trade in Southwestern Virginia," in *Environmental History and the American South: A Reader*, ed. Paul Sutter and Christopher J. Manganiello (Athens: University of Georgia Press, 2009), 270.

18. Shawn William Miller, *An Environmental History of Latin America* (New York: Cambridge University Press, 2007), 70.

19. Bill Gammage, "Plain Facts: Tasmania under Aboriginal Management," *Landscape Research* 33(2) (2008): 241–254.

20. World War Four Report, "Peru: Amazon Uprising Spreads," last modified June 7, 2009, accessed January 4, 2013, http://ww4report.com/node/7411.

21. Alfred Crosby, *Ecological Imperialism: The Biological Expansion of Europe, 900–1900* (Cambridge: Cambridge University Press, 1986).

22. Madhav Gadgil and Ramachandra Guha, *This Fissured Land: An Ecological History of India* (Oxford: Oxford University Press, 1997).

23. Karl Marx, *Early Writings* (Harmondsworth: Penguin, 1977), 239.

24. E. P. Thompson, *Customs in Common* (Harmondsworth: Penguin, 1991), 180–181.

25. John Clare, *A Champion for the Poor: Political Verse and Prose* (Manchester: Carcanet, 2000), 47.

26. R. Paul, "A Language That Is Ever Green": The Poetry and Ecology of John Clare," *Modernaspråk* 105(2) (2011): 28.

27. Peter Linebaugh, *The Magna Carta Manifesto: Liberties and Commons for All* (Berkeley: University of California Press, 2008), 31.

28. Christopher Hill, *Winstanley: "The Law of Freedom" and Other Writings* (Cambridge: Cambridge University Press, 1973), 84.

29. Peter Linebaugh and Marcus Rediker, *The Many-Headed Hydra: The Hidden History of the Revolutionary Atlantic* (London: Verso, 2002).

30. Ben Maddison, "Radical Commons Discourse and the Challenges of Colonialism," *Radical History Review* 108 (2010): 29–48.

31. Michael Hardt and Antonio Negri, *Empire* (Cambridge, Mass.: Harvard University Press, 2000), 303.

32. Ibid.

33. Walter Mignolo, "The Communal and the Decolonial," last modified 2009, accessed January 4, 2013, http://turbulence.org.uk/turbulence-5/decolonial.

34. Maddison, "Radical Commons Discourse and the Challenges of Colonialism."

35. BBC, "Watercress Thieves Target River Kennet in Hungerford," last modified August 30, 2011, accessed January 4, 2013, http://www.bbc.co.uk/news/uk-england-berkshire-14677554.

36. Christopher Caldwell, "John Clare, Peasant, Lunatic, Poet," *Slate*, last modified August 30, 2011, accessed January 10, 2013, http://www.slate.com/articles/arts/books/2003/10/man_out_of_time.html.

37. Charles Tilly, *Popular Contention in Great Britain, 1758–1834* (Cambridge, Mass.: Harvard University Press, 1995).

38. Thompson, *Customs in Common*, 104.

39. Jane Humphries, "Enclosures, Common Rights, and Women: The Proletarianization of Families in the Late Eighteenth and Early Nineteenth Centuries," *Journal of Economic History* 50(1) (1990): 17–42.

40. Silvia Federici, *Caliban and the Witch: Women, the Body and Primitive Accumulation* (New York: Autonomedia, 2004), 73–74.

41. South London Radical History Group, *Down with the Fences! Battles for the Commons in South London* (London: Past Tense, 2004).

42. Stephanie Boyd, "Brutality in Bagua," *New Internationalist* blog, last modified June 17, 2009, accessed January 4, 2013, http://www.newint.org/blog/editors/2009/06/17/brutality-in-bagua.

43. Christopher Rodgers, Margherita Pieraccini, Eleanor A. Straughton, and Angus Winchester, *Contested Common Land: Environmental Governance Past and Present* (London: Earthscan, 2010), 1.

44. Massimo De Angelis and Stavros Stavrides, "On the Commons: A Public Interview with Massimo De Angelis and Stavros Stavrides," *E-flux* 17 (June 2010): 1.

45. Malcolm Chase, *"The People's Farm": English Radical Agrarianism, 1775–1840* (Oxford: Clarendon Press, 1988), 180.

46. Nate Harrison, *"Can I Get an Amen,"* 2004, Web, http://nkhstudio.com/pages/popup_amen.html.

4   Questions for Good Ancestors

1. Michael Leroy Oberg, "Good Neighbors: The Onondagas and the Fort Schuyler Treaty of September 1788," *New York History* 88(4) (2007): 391.

2. Jared Diamond, *Collapse: How Societies Choose to Fail or Survive* (London: Penguin, 2006), 114.

3. Terry Hunt and Carl Lipo, *The Statues That Walked: Unraveling the Mystery of Easter Island* (New York: Free Press, 2011).

4. Benny Peiser, "From Genocide to Ecocide: The Rape of Rapa Nui," *Energy & Environment* 16(3) (2005): 513–540.

5. Bjørn Lomborg, *The Skeptical Environmentalist: Measuring the Real State of the World* (Cambridge: Cambridge University Press, 2001).

6. Martin Richardson, *Globalisation and International Trade Liberalisation: Continuity and Change* (Cheltenham: Edward Elgar, 2000), 127.

7. Hayden White, *Metahistory: The Historical Imagination in Nineteenth-Century Europe* (Baltimore: Johns Hopkins University Press, 1973).

8. Thomas Pynchon, *Gravity's Rainbow* (London: Vintage, 2000), 299.

9. E. P. Thompson, *Customs in Common* (Harmondsworth: Penguin, 1991), 114.

10. Robert Netting, *Balancing on an Alp: Ecological Change and Continuity in a Swiss Mountain Community* (Cambridge: Cambridge University Press, 1981).

11. Christopher Hannibal-Paci, "Lake Sturgeon: The Historical Geography of Lake Winnipeg Fishery Commons," paper presented at Crossing Boundaries, the Seventh Biennial Conference of the International Association for the Study of Common Property, Vancouver, British Columbia, Canada, June 10–14, 1998, accessed January 4, 2013, http://dlc.dlib.indiana.edu/dlc/handle/10535/2105.

12. William Cronon, *Changes in the Land: Indians, Colonists, and the Ecology of New England* (New York: Hill and Wang, 1983).

13. Mark Bowden, Graham Brown, and Nicky Smith, *An Archaeology of Town Commons* (Swindon, UK: English Heritage, 2009).

14. Larry Lohmann, "Carbon Trading, Climate Justice and the Production of Ignorance: Ten Examples," *Development* 51(3) (1937): 359–365.

15. Elinor Ostrom, "A Polycentric Approach for Coping with Climate Change," background paper to the 2010 World Development Report, World Bank, Washington, D.C., 2009.

16. Ibid., 38.

17. Charles Lane, "Barabaig Natural Resource Management: Sustainable Land Use under Threat of Destruction," Discussion Paper 12, United Nations Research Institute for Social Development, 1990, 8.

18. Minority Rights Group, "Barabaig," last modified 2005, accessed January 4, 2013, http://www.minorityrights.org/4784/united-repub lic-of-tanzania/barabaig.html.

19. Kenneth R. Olwig, "Globalism and the Enclosure of the Landscape Commons," Landscape Archaeology and Ecology 8 (2010): 154–163, 161.

20. Michael Hardt and Antonio Negri, Commonwealth (Cambridge, Mass.: Harvard University Press, 2009), 7.

21. Yochai Benkler, "'Sharing Nicely': On Shareable Goods and the Emergence of Sharing as a Modality of Economic Production," Yale Law Journal 114 (2005): 273–358.

22. Rachel Botsman and Roo Rogers, What's Mine Is Yours: The Rise of Collaborative Consumption (London: Harper Collins, 2010).

23. Netting, Balancing on an Alp, 24.

24. David Frank, J. B. McLachlan: A Biography (Toronto: James Lorimer, 1999), 73.

25. Silke Helfrich, Rainer Kuhlen, Wolfgang Sachs, and Christian Siefkes. The Commons: Prosperity by Sharing (Berlin: Heinrich Böll Foundation, 2010).

26. Heinrich Böll Foundation, "Commons," last modified 2010, accessed January 4, 2013, http://www.boell.de/economysocial/economy/economy-commons-10451.html.

27. Mining and Indigenous Rights in the Cordillera del Condor of Peru, "Our War against the Crab," last modified 2009, accessed January 4, 2013, http://odecofroc.blogspot.co.uk/p/7.html.

28. Paul Lafargue, Selected Marxist Writings of Paul Lafargue (Berkeley, Calif.: Center for Socialist History, 1984), 44.

29. Teodor Shanin, Late Marx and the Russian Road: Marx and "the Peripheries of Capitalism" (New York: Monthly Review Press, 1983), 124.

30. Hilary Wainwright and Dave Elliott, *The Lucas Plan: A New Trade Unionism in the Making?* (London: Allison and Busby, 1982).

31. Gilles Deleuze and Félix Guattari, *A Thousand Plateaus: Capitalism and Schizophrenia* (London: Continuum, 1987), 191.

32. Jeanette Neeson, *Commoners: Common Right, Enclosure and Social Change in England, 1700–1820* (Cambridge: Cambridge University Press, 1993), 328.

33. Hardt and Negri, *Commonwealth.*

34. Personal comment.

35. Jay Walljasper, "Fifty-one (Mostly) Simple Ways to Spark a Commons Revolution," *On the Commons*, last modified April 25, 2011, accessed January 4, 2013, http://www.onthecommons.org/magazine/51-mostly-simple-ways-spark-commons-revolution.

36. Elinor Ostrom, "No Common Solution for Development Issues, Ostrom Tells Govt," interview with Amitabh Sinha, *Indian Express*, January 7, 2011.

37. Aaron Peters, "The Movement That Needs No Name," *Open Democracy*, last modified July 1, 2011, accessed January 4, 2013, http://www.opendemocracy.net/ourkingdom/aaron-peters/movement-that-needs-no-name.

38. Eric S. Raymond, *The Cathedral and the Bazaar: Musings on Linux and Open Source by an Accidental Revolutionary* (Cambridge, Mass.: O'Reilly, 1999).

39. Iain Bruce, *The Real Venezuela: Making Socialism in the Twenty-First Century* (London: Pluto, 2008), 161.

40. Ralph H. Lutts, "Like Manna from God: The American Chestnut Trade in Southwestern Virginia," in *Environmental History and the American South: A Reader*, ed. Paul Sutter and Christopher J. Manganiello (Athens: University of Georgia Press, 2009).

41. Oliver Rackham, *The History of the British Countryside* (London: Dent, 1986), 287.

42. Jules Verne, *Journey to the Centre of the Earth* (London: Wordsworth Editions, 1996), 46.

43. Douglas Weiner, *Models of Nature: Ecology, Conservation and Cultural Revolution in Soviet Russia* (Pittsburgh, Pa.: University of Pittsburgh Press, 2000).

44. Mancur Olson, *Power and Prosperity: Outgrowing Communist and Capitalist Dictatorships* (New York: Basic Books, 2000).

45. Elinor Ostrom, "The Challenge of Common-Pool Resources," *Environment: Science and Policy for Sustainable Development* 50(4) (2008): 13.

46. Elinor Ostrom, "Crafting Rules to Sustain Resources," speech delivered to the American Academy of Political and Social Science, last modified 2008, accessed January 4, 2013, http://www.aapss.org/news/2008/05/29/crafting-rules-to-sustain-resources.

47. William N. Fenton, *The Great Law and the Longhouse: A Political History of the Iroquois Confederacy* (Norman: University of Oklahoma Press, 1998).

48. Glenn Morris, "For the Next Seven Generations: Indigenous Americans and Communalism," Fellowship for Intentional Community, last modified 1996, accessed January 4, 2013, http://www.ic.org/pnp/cdir/1995/30morris.php.

49. Kathryn Newfont, *Blue Ridge Commons: Environmental Activism and Forest History in Western North Carolina* (Athens: University of Georgia Press, 2012), 310.

50. Cronon, *Changes in the Land*.

51. Colin Scott and Monica Mulrennan, "Connection to Land and Sea at Erub, Torres Strait," last modified 1998, accessed January 4, 1998, http://dlc.dlib.indiana.edu/dlc/bitstream/handle/10535/1844/scotmulr.pdf?sequence=1.

Selected Readings on the Commons

Ashbrook, Kate, and Nicola Hodgson. *Finding Common Ground.* Henley-on-Thames, UK: Open Spaces Society, 2010.

Bardhan, Pranab, and Isha Ray. *Contested Commons: Conversations between Economists and Anthropologists.* Oxford: Blackwell, 2008.

Benkler, Yochai. *The Wealth of Networks: How Social Production Transforms Markets and Freedom.* London: Yale University Press, 2006.

Bollier, David, and Silke Helfrich, eds. *The Wealth of the Commons.* Amherst, Mass.: Levellers Press, 2012.

Cronon, William. *Changes in the Land: Indians, Colonists, and the Ecology of New England.* New York: Hill and Wang, 1983.

de Moor, Martina, Leigh Shaw-Taylor, and Paul Warde, eds. *The Management of Common Land in North West Europe, c. 1500–1850.* Turnhout, Belgium: Brepols, 2002.

Hardt, Michael, and Antonio Negri. *Empire.* Cambridge, Mass.: Harvard University Press, 2000.

Linebaugh, Peter. *The Magna Carta Manifesto: Liberties and Commons for All.* Berkeley: University of California Press, 2008.

Neeson, Jeanette. *Commoners: Common Right, Enclosure and Social Change in England, 1700–1820.* Cambridge: Cambridge University Press, 1993.

Netting, Robert. *Balancing on an Alp: Ecological Change and Continuity in a Swiss Mountain Community.* Cambridge: Cambridge University Press, 1981.

Newfont, Kathryn. *Blue Ridge Commons: Environmental Activism and Forest History in Western North Carolina.* Athens: University of Georgia Press, 2012.

Oosthuizen, Susan. "Archaeology, Common Rights and the Origins of Anglo-Saxon Identity." *Early Medieval Europe* 19 (2) (2011): 153–181.

Ostrom, Elinor. *Governing the Commons: The Evolution of Institutions for Collective Action.* Cambridge: Cambridge University Press, 1990.

Ostrom, Elinor, Roy Gardner, and James Walker. *Rules, Games, and Common-Pool Resources.* Ann Arbor: University of Michigan Press, 1994.

Rodgers, Christopher, Margherita Pieraccini, Eleanor A. Straughton, and Angus Winchester. *Contested Common Land: Environmental Governance Past and Present.* London: Earthscan, 2010.

Stayer, James. *The German Peasant's War and Anabaptist Community of Goods.* Montreal: McGill-Queen's University Press, 1994.

Strang, Veronica. *Uncommon Ground: Cultural Landscapes and Environmental Values.* Oxford: Berg, 1997.

Thompson, E. P. *Customs in Common.* Harmondsworth, UK: Penguin, 1991.

Wade, Robert. *Village Republics: Economic Conditions for Collective Action in South India.* Cambridge: Cambridge University Press, 1988.

Index

Printed in the United States
by Baker & Taylor Publisher Services